THE
VERY
SMALL
GARDEN

THE VERY SMALL GARDEN

Martin Baxendale

SOUVENIR
PRESS

First published 1986 by Souvenir Press Ltd,
43 Great Russell Street, London WC1B 3PA
and simultaneously in Canada

ISBN 0 285 62736 8

Photoset in Great Britain by
Rowland Phototypesetting Ltd,
Bury St Edmunds, Suffolk and
printed in Great Britain by
William Clowes Ltd,
Beccles, Suffolk

Contents

Preface

Written with first-time gardeners particularly in mind, the following chapters offer ideas and planting suggestions that should be of interest to anyone working to create a beautiful garden in a restricted space.

How to make the most of the available space, how to create the best overall effect, and what to plant where growing room is scarce and cramped —these are the most important and urgent questions facing the owners of small gardens, and especially first-time house buyers enjoying a garden of their own as a new and exciting adventure. The main aim of this book is to offer some straightforward answers to these and other vital basic questions.

Throughout the book I return again and again to the theme of cramming in as many plants as possible, in as great a variety as possible. In my view, this is the very essence of good gardening in a restricted space; to create a garden packed so full of beautiful and interesting plants that to explore it fully takes as long as a stroll through a larger garden.

Choosing neat-growing plants is an essential part of this maximum-interest-from-the-minimum-space philosophy. You will find, therefore, that a large proportion of the book has been devoted to detailed descriptions and planting suggestions for a wide range of suitable plants —from trees to tiny alpines. Inevitably, many of these are personal favourites of mine, but my hope is that they will soon become favourites of yours, too.

Most of the basic practical problems facing owners of small gardens are tackled, but technical gardening practices like pruning, propagation and so forth fall outside the scope of this book. These skills may be quickly picked up from more general gardening manuals and encyclopaedias. My concern here is to help you get the most out of your available space, turning what may look like an unpromising square plot into a little wonderland.

M.B.

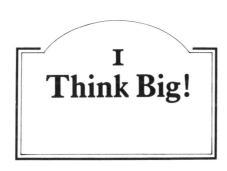

I
Think Big!

Mention small gardens to some people and they assume that you are talking about anything up to an acre, or even more; but the small gardens that most of us know all too well are more likely to be measured in a few metres or, at most, in tiny fractions of an acre.

When I talk about small gardens, I really do mean small: narrow strips of lawn and border, tiny housing estate plots and claustrophobic courtyards; the very smallest gardens where finding room for even a single tree can sometimes pose problems (or even prove quite impossible).

All the gardens I have owned so far have been decidedly on the small side. The first, and the most unforgettable, was a cell-like courtyard barely six metres from corner to corner, with the towering backs of three-storey town houses crowding in on all sides like gloomy urban cliffs. That was my 'back garden'; as for the 'front garden', I could reach out from my window and open the gate for visitors without even having to set foot out of doors!

I had been used to the luxury of far more spacious gardening with my mother and father, and at first glance my pocket-handkerchief plot looked quite depressing. Yet in that shady patch of stony clay I managed to grow a wide range of alpine plants, a selection of the neater herbaceous perennials, several small shrubs, climbers, a small tree, bulbs galore, a few annuals for added summer colour, some fruit and even the occasional lettuce or tomato; and there was still room for a patch of grass. Looking back, I think I got as much enjoyment out of that secluded little 'backyard' as any garden since; and I certainly learned a lot about making the most of very little and

squeezing a quart into a pint pot, which is what making a small garden is all about.

Over the years I have also learnt not to be too modest about my small-scale gardens, because what makes a garden exciting is not sheer size alone, but what is in it and what has been done with it. All too often people say to me: 'Oh, you don't want to see my garden . . . it's so tiny.' Yet the smallest of gardens can be beautiful and interesting if the owner sets his or her heart on making it so, and is prepared to experiment, learn and use a little imagination.

Many gardeners have worked miracles in cramped conditions, creating tiny wonderlands that are as much a delight to explore in their own way as the grandest country estates: little gardens crammed with plants as beautiful and enthralling as you could wish to see. And anyone who creates a fascinating and lovely small garden certainly deserves at least as much praise as the most successful of large-scale gardeners, if not more.

There is no doubt that the best way to create an interesting garden is to be adventurous in both choice of plants and garden layout. Obviously there is nothing more boring, both for yourself and for visitors, than a garden filled with exactly the same things that everyone else in the street is growing.

The keen gardener will not just settle for what the local garden centre has to offer. He or she will also want to explore other nurseries and garden centres and search through mail-order catalogues and books, looking for those less common things that make all the difference between the dull sameness that so often pervades small gardens and a novelty and beauty that will draw gasps of delight from owner and visitor alike; the plants that will make people exclaim, 'Oh, that's lovely!' instead of simply, 'Oh, yes. I have that.' Nowhere is this diversity more important than in a small garden, where even the occasional adventurous choice can transform the entire scene.

Nor should any gardener, even the most inexperienced beginner, be too quickly put off a plant, simply because it is labelled by the experts as 'difficult'. If everyone grew the easiest plants, then our gardens would definitely become boring and monotonous; a small garden can grow the loveliest of plants just as well as the largest one. If you fancy a plant but have heard that it is not particularly easy, then check the books and find out just what it needs to succeed; if you do not try it, you may miss out on the gardening thrill of a lifetime.

For example, lilies have a reputation for being difficult to please. Yet there are some, like the deliciously fragrant white and wine-red trumpet-flowered *Lilium regale*, which are almost as easy to grow as daffodils, given a well-drained position. It is this kind of stunning plant that will really make a garden stand out from its neighbours and turn even the smallest plot into the exciting adventure that it ought to be.

In a tiny garden, the main aim should always be to cram in as many of the best and most beautiful plants as possible; where space is at a premium, there is no room for the second-rate or for plants which give only a half-hearted return for their keep. It may sound hard, but anything which refuses to do well or make a decent showing, despite the gardener's utmost care, is best replaced with something better; the garden will benefit in the long run. Anything which offers more than one good feature, like a flowering display coupled with handsome foliage, autumn colour, berries or colourful spring shoots, is particularly valuable in a small space. Of course there should always be a place for the favourite 'ordinary' plant, the plant that everyone loves (gardening snobbery is an obnoxious vice); but it should preferably be a good variety, very free-flowering and very long-flowering. 'Nothing but the best' would be a good motto for the small-scale gardener.

Another important point, of course, is to aim for a succession of colour and interest throughout the year, so that there is always something to see and admire in every season.

Naturally, the main display should come in spring and summer, when the garden will be most frequently in use and the weather warm enough to permit leisurely enjoyment of the plants and flowers. But there should always be at least a few plants specifically chosen to keep the view from the house interesting and colourful even in the coldest months; or, better still, interesting enough to entice the reluctant gardener outside for a breath of fresh air and a poke around, to see how things are doing and to carry out a few small gardening chores.

Where space is strictly limited, it is not easy to squeeze in masses of plants for every season of the year, but do your best. Every time you plant a few things for spring and summer, stop and think about balancing the scales a little with the odd plant or bulb for autumn or winter; you will find that you need only a few, because one flower during the bleak months is worth a hundred in June or July.

I have already mentioned plants with more than one attractive feature, and if these offer their different attractions in separate seasons (like spring or summer flowers followed by autumn foliage tints or berries), then they are doubly useful. And do not forget that autumn is not the only time when many shrubs, trees and plants produce bright leaf colourings: quite a few give us the double bonus of flowers plus colourful spring foliage. In the chapters that follow, these two-season plants will be highlighted and strongly recommended.

Evergreen plants and shrubs are of course vital, acting as screens and filling the garden with handsome and sometimes colourful foliage throughout the year. They prevent the view from becoming too bare and desolate when herbaceous and deciduous things take their winter rest. Bulbs, too, are a must; they can give us flowers

A particularly fine white Helleborus orientalis *form, flowering in late winter. The handsome leaves provide interest throughout the year.*

for every season, and they are great space-savers when interplanted amongst other things and underplanted beneath shrubs and trees. A great many are so tiny that they take up little room in return for a superb patch of colour and are ideal for restricted spaces; and the same goes for the neater species and varieties of rock plant, dozens of which can be housed in just a few square feet of soil where they will provide immense interest and enchanting early flowers.

Remember also that fragrance plays an important role in the garden, and particularly in the small garden; search out plants with strongly scented flowers that will double the enjoyment to be had from a tiny area.

Having ensured some interest and colour in all seasons, the keen gardener will probably also want to make sure that his or her main summer display is going to be a magnificent and long-lasting affair, non-stop from the last days of spring through to the first autumn mists. This is not easy to achieve even in a large garden, let alone where space is at a premium; and the owner of a very small garden has to accept that although there will be times when the display reaches a stunning peak, there will also be in-between periods which are not quite so colourful.

Many gardeners use annuals and tender bedding plants for additional summer colour, but it is important to remember that these only provide a temporary boost to the garden display. They must go in the autumn (annuals to the compost heap and tender bedding plants into frost-free winter storage). Rely too heavily on them, and you will only find yourself with large and ugly patches of bare earth later on; and then you will have to start putting in spring bedding plants as replacements, followed by more summer annuals, and so on, year after year; all a great deal of trouble, and think of all those wasted empty gaps in your tiny garden where every inch of soil is valuable. Use annuals by all means, and tender bedding plants if you can store them over the winter; but do not expect them to be the answer to all your problems. They are useful for filling gaps and providing extra colour in the border and in window boxes, hanging baskets and so forth; but the backbone of the garden is best made up of plants that are permanent and comparatively trouble-free.

Plenty of shrubs and perennials offer the gardener as long-lasting and as bright a display as any annual, and if you want non-stop summer colour (and lots of it) then try to include at least some of these in the garden plan. To mention just a few of my favourites, I can heartily recommend the following easy plants: shrubby potentillas, crocosmias, *Geranium sanguineum*, perennial oenotheras, *Viola cornuta*, helianthemums, campanulas, the superb pink mallow-flowered *Lavatera olbia* 'Rosea', primroses and polyanthus (for spring) and hardy fuchsias (for late summer and autumn).

It is a good idea to choose plants specifically to bloom in different periods of the summer. Make sure you have a few for early summer, more to continue the show into late July and August, and one or two to see you through to autumn. Always check flowering times carefully, and bear them in mind as part of your garden planning.

However, as any gardener knows (or soon finds out), merely choosing lovely plants will not make a garden; it also needs to be thoughtfully laid out to add to the interest, and that means planning, even on a small scale. In a large garden you can get away with having seasonal dull spots, some borders bursting with summer flowers and others that are really colourful only in spring or autumn. Where planting space is limited, it is better to spread your summer colour evenly around the garden, well mixed with plants for autumn, winter and spring, so that you do not have large blank areas at any time of the year. This may sound very basic, but it all takes a fair amount of thinking-through which is easily overlooked in the enthusiastic rush to start planting.

Then there is the question of overall garden design and layout, the problems of hiding ugly features and views, and thinking up ideas which will help you to squeeze in a few extra plants. So, no matter whether your garden covers half an acre or a few square yards, there is a lot of thinking to be done before getting busy with spade and trowel.

In fact, if there is one golden rule that is truer of small gardens than any others, it is 'think before you plant'; and, at the same time, you should also 'think big'. Your garden may be small by some people's standards, but there is a lot you can do with it and a great deal of pleasure to be had from it; tackle it with the same enthusiasm and pride that you would apply to a larger garden, and it will repay you a hundredfold. Naturally, you cannot do everything at once, but then no gardener ever does. If you are starting on a new garden, you can have fun working out a long-term plan of campaign which may take several seasons to complete. Even in an apparently 'finished' garden (if such a thing can exist) there is always room for improvement, which can be carried out stage by stage over the years.

Before looking more closely at garden layout and plant selection, I'd like to mention one more point that will help you to get the most from a small garden. Try if you can to become truly interested in and involved with the plants, not just as so much outdoor decoration but as living things. The greatest gardeners (and, more importantly, those who seem to have derived the greatest pleasure from gardening) have always been those who took the closest possible interest in their plants; the gardeners who wanted to know not just what colour the flowers would be, but everything there was to know about the little pieces of living natural history that they were cultivating: where the plants originate from, why they grow as they do, how they propagate themselves (and how we can help!), and much more.

Like the ornithologist who wants to learn more about birds than their mere names, the really keen gardener will find that half the fascination of the hobby lies in reading and accumulating knowledge, some of it useful in a practical way and much of it quite simply enthralling. Every plant in the garden has a tale to tell of the natural and human world, covering such wide-ranging subjects as botany, geography, adaptation and survival, social and economic history, plant collection in the wild, hybridisation, gardening history and a great deal more. It is all out there in the garden, and in the books in the local library and shops.

The person who ignores this side of gardening and sees only the colourful flowers, may greatly enjoy his or her garden and get immense pleasure from it—but not as much as the gardener with an inquisitive mind and a thirst for knowledge.

2
Doing it in Style

Whether you are tackling a completely new plot or thinking about improving or renovating an existing garden, one of the first things to decide is what sort of style you would like to aim for —formal, informal, cottage garden, etc.— because naturally everything else will stem from this.

Formal layouts, with their geometrical shapes and contrived bedding schemes, seldom fit happily into very small gardens. They tend to seem what they are: pale imitations of the grander schemes seen in parks and great gardens (which is where they should remain, on the kind of scale for which they were devised). In any case, the straight lines and strictly regimented beds of a formal design will only emphasise the rectangular or square shape of the average small garden, making it seem even more boxed-in. A good design should do the exact opposite, disguising the straight boundaries and breaking up the square look to create a softer and more interesting view.

To achieve this, the style must be informal; or perhaps casual might be an even better description; curving borders and meandering paths with few straight lines, and mixed plantings of shrubs, hardy perennials, bulbs and annuals; all closely planted and growing together into an almost solid mass of foliage and flower colour.

Adopting a casual and mixed planting style like this is also the best way to squeeze a lot of plants (and therefore a lot of colour and interest) into a small area. It is virtually a cottage garden approach, and one that I like very much for its luxuriant and easy-going effect. Some people might argue that the garden will acquire an over-crowded appearance, but if you are trying to cram a lot of exciting plants into a tiny space, then a little overcrowding is inevitable and, as far as I am concerned, does no harm. Plants grow packed together in the wild, intermingling and even growing through one another, so why should they not be allowed to do the same in the garden?

If the end result is a rather haphazard, luxuriant and increasingly 'natural' appearance, that is nothing to complain about. So many of us are trapped amongst the concrete and bricks of our towns and cities for so much of the time that, apart from parks, our gardens are our main link with the natural world; why twist and warp them into the very urban uniformity and orderliness from which we like to escape, when with a relaxed approach our gardens can bring more of that sought-after natural look right to our doorsteps?

A crowded, even 'overgrown', garden also attracts much more wildlife. Thick masses of evergreen shrubs will appeal more to birds than regimented rows of winter-bare bush roses, and a wide range of closely-planted flowers will draw in masses of butterflies and bees. If you are lucky, a friendly toad might be attracted by your densely-packed, shady borders (particularly if you have a small pond) and will keep the slugs down for you, by way of rent.

Of course, an informal garden style does not have to be complete anarchy. There should be purpose to the plantings; an overall scheme with

'Cottage garden style': the author's garden in spring. This new garden was planted just twelve months before the photograph was taken – close planting certainly produces an immediate effect.

an infinite number of possible variations, ranging from the almost totally wild garden, through simple arrangements of grass and plant-filled borders, to intricate designs involving raised beds, retaining walls, patios, pools, or whatever takes your fancy.

I am not going to lay down lots of 'do' and 'don't' rules on garden design, because my basic philosophy on gardening is: 'almost anything goes; if you want to try out an idea then go ahead. If you are pleased with it, do not worry too much about what other people might say; only if you find that most of your visitors hate it should you perhaps think again.' But do, whatever your personal tastes, be a little 'laid back' in your approach, keeping your designs and plans as casual and simple as possible, rather than going for anything too contrived or fussy. Most importantly, do not be afraid to cram the plants in —lots of them, and in as wide a range as possible.

I mentioned mixed plantings of shrubs and perennials as an essential part of a casual gardening style. There is no doubt that this is the most satisfactory way to plant beds and borders in small gardens, rather than trying to create separate shrubberies, rose beds, herbaceous borders, bedding displays and so forth. Segregate the plants strictly into groups of the same type and you will inevitably end up with large bare patches when the non-evergreens lose their leaves in autumn and the bedding plants are over.

Thoroughly mix all kinds of plants together, and the result is quite different. Evergreen shrubs and perennials, scattered throughout the borders, provide year-round foliage everywhere; autumn, winter and spring bulbs fill the gaps when deciduous plants die down; and when the bulbs in turn disappear below ground in late spring, the herbaceous plants are coming up to take over again, accompanied by summer bulbs and also a few annuals or tender bedding plants for extra colour, if you wish; and so it goes on, with few chances of large gaps in the display.

In the following chapter I shall look in greater detail at the way such mixed plantings can help the gardener to squeeze in more plants to the square yard; I shall also discuss further space-saving and problem-solving ideas and plans for the very small garden.

3
Making the Most of a Small Garden

Making plans

Once you have decided on the overall 'look' that you want to achieve in the garden, it is time to start detailed planning. The best way to do this, even if you are only making minor changes or improvements, is on paper.

Draw a map of the garden (or proposed garden) with everything to scale, pacing out distances to make sure you get the dimensions exactly right. Take the map outside and mark down as much detail as possible, including the bad points. Note down any ugly features like tumbledown sheds, dilapidated walls or fences, manhole covers or unsightly views outside the garden that you might want to cover up or screen; mark exposed boundaries that might need hedging for wind protection and privacy; map the sunny areas and the shady corners; note areas that are particularly damp, or dry and stony, and slopes that might benefit from terracing with a retaining wall.

At the same time, draw in any attractive features or views that you would like to retain, that you do not want to become hidden behind trees or large shrubs planted in the wrong place.

Only after doing this ground-work should you start to draw up your plans, continually taking more strolls outside to refresh your memory, check out ideas and views, try out measurements and generally reconsider.

Of course, in very small gardens there is a limit to what can be done in the way of layout. So, to reiterate what I said in the last chapter, keep your plans simple and bold, remembering that the ultimate aim is to improve the outlook and add interest without creating a clutter of oddly-shaped and fussy little beds and features. Better

to have just one or two large borders or beds if space is severely limited, and make these real showpieces.

The vast majority of small gardens are square or rectangular in shape, and trying to disguise this will improve the look of the garden more than almost anything else. A great deal can be done to this end by creating curved borders, rather than having them all straight-edged and rectangular. But do make the curves long and sweeping, not full of sharp kinks and wriggles which will look ridiculously artificial and which, as a lawn edging, will prove awkward to mow around. In the tiniest spaces, in any case, there may be room for only one or two curves.

Considerably widening the borders in one or two places, so that they protrude into the lawn (if you have one!) in curving bulges or peninsulas, will further break up the square or rectangular look; but, once again, do not overdo this in a very small garden.

If you do decide to broaden the borders here and there, plan the curves alternately on each side of the garden in a staggered effect; this will create a very slightly meandering or winding view up the centre, which will distract the eye from the straight boundaries. Never have two wide sections of border bulging out into the lawn from opposite sides at exactly the same point, almost pinching the lawn in two. In the very tiniest of town gardens there may not even be room to do this sort of thing, in which case settle for simple sweeping shapes.

Borders which curve out towards the centre of the garden are particularly useful if you can create little nooks behind them—tiny areas cut off from the immediate view like compartments which add to the interest of the garden walk (particularly if these 'hidden' areas house an especially interesting feature or group of plants). The same effect can be achieved with low hedges, low walls, raised beds with retaining walls, or a trellis covered with climbing plants; but here again, you cannot divide up a tiny garden too much without making it seem cramped and claustrophobic, so take care.

Some garden designers play around with layouts for lawns, paths and beds based on circles, triangles and all kinds of other shapes, but these always seem to introduce a note that is too formal and contrived for my taste.

If, for example, you like the idea of a circular lawn or paved area surrounded by curving beds on all sides, then by all means try it. Something like this can work quite well in a tiny square garden, but once again keep it simple. Some of the layouts that I have seen, where the lawn and beds are a series of linked circles, might be decidedly over the top on a very small scale; this sort of design requires enough space for the linked circles all to be of a reasonable size, otherwise the whole effect starts to become extremely fussy and artificial.

These are all very general observations and suggestions; I feel that there is little point in my setting out two or three sample 'ideal' garden layouts, complete in every detail, because every garden poses its own problems, limitations and possibilities.

In any case, the best way to pick up ideas is not from pretty drawings and plans which may look superb on paper but disappointing when you try to make them fit your particular size and shape of garden. If you need inspiration, apart from the basic guidelines given, nothing beats looking at other gardens 'in the flesh'; visit gardens open to the public in your area (especially the smaller ones) and keep your eyes peeled for attractive layouts in private gardens that you might pass in the street. But whatever you finally decide on, remember to keep it simple.

The importance of grass
A couple of paragraphs back, I mentioned lawns and paving in the same sentence, as alternative central features for the small garden, and it has to be admitted that some gardens are so tiny that finding space for even the smallest patch of grass is a real problem.

In this situation, paved and gravelled areas are the obvious options and they really can look very attractive, particularly with a few low-growing carpeting plants sprouting through the gravel or from the gaps between the slabs. Some of the stronger-growing alpine plants are perfect for this sort of situation, and so are various aromatic plants like the thymes, which fill the air with spicy fragrances when inadvertently stepped on; I shall suggest some suitable choices in Chapter Seven.

However, I must put in a strong plea for grass, even where space is strictly limited. Attractive as paving and gravel can be, nothing can really replace a patch of cool green turf as the ideal centre-point to a garden, just as nothing beats a fire as the focal-point of a room; and in a town or city garden, where the main desire is surely to soften the effects of the surrounding brick, stone or concrete, to introduce too much paving or gravel is obviously a step in the wrong direction.

Even if your garden is measured in only a few metres, do try to find room for at least a little grass; it adds so much to the scene in winter when we need all the greenery we can get; and it is so much cooler and more pleasant to walk and sit on during summer than dusty paving or gravel—even if it is only just large enough for a deckchair or two.

Apart from space, the main problems with lawns in small gardens in towns and cities are excessive shade from surrounding buildings and poorly-drained clay soils. But these can be overcome.

Very shady areas can be sown with one of the grass seed mixtures sold in garden shops specifically to grow well in shade, and existing lawns can be over-sown with the same seed mix. Improving the soil will also help grass to thrive in shade, and this is particularly important on clay. Before sowing new lawns, dig in peat and coarse sand to lighten heavy soil and improve the drainage, plus a pre-seeding lawn fertiliser; peat is of course the easiest soil-improving material to buy in towns and cities, although you may also be able to get spent mushroom compost which is both cheap and very good. Should the new lawn site be on very dry, sandy or stony ground, adding peat and fertiliser will help, but of course the sand will not be needed. And existing lawns can also be improved—damp, mossy lawns by raking in peat and coarse sand, and dry patches by raking in peat alone (and feeding with lawn fertiliser to boost summer growth).

Coping with shade

Having mentioned one of the problems of shade (all too common in crowded urban gardens) this is probably a good place to discuss the subject further, since it can have such a vital bearing on garden planning and planting.

When making your plans for the garden, one of the first things to do is to locate the sunniest spot for sitting out in summer, and then to ensure that any new tall shrubs or trees you put in will not cast too much shade over this area. Apart from this, shade is not really as much of a problem as you might think, because there are plenty of plants which will happily grow without full sun; even the most enclosed garden should receive at least some sunshine during the summer when the sun is high in the sky.

That last point is worth bearing in mind when choosing plants for gloomy corners (or for a gloomy garden). What looks like a very shady garden in autumn, winter or spring may—when the sun rises higher in the summer sky and blazes down mercilessly from directly overhead—become a real sun-trap from June to August. You could fill a dimly-lit bed in spring with plants that love shade and moisture, only to find that later in the year they are receiving much more sun than you had expected—or they can tolerate. This is especially important if you have just taken over a new garden and are not aware of how the shade moves round during the day and over the seasons.

On the other hand, you might move into a new garden in July and find that you have a very hot, sunny area or a wall which seems ideal for plants, shrubs and climbers that require plenty of sun to grow and flower well; but you could discover later that it only receives sunlight for a few short weeks in mid-summer, being overshadowed by surrounding buildings for the rest of the year.

No one can really get to know a garden well until at least one full gardening year has been experienced in it. Naturally, you cannot wait indefinitely to start planting, but a little caution and patience will pay in the end, especially if you are planning major new planting schemes, or if you intend putting in plants which are slightly tender, or fussy about soil and situation. Delaying some of your planting plans for a season or two, to gain experience of winter or summer conditions, never does any harm; even if it is only a matter of waiting to plant in autumn instead of spring (to see what the garden is like in summer) or putting off autumn plantings until the following spring (when you will have seen how winter affects the garden).

Waiting a season or two before making major changes or doing large-scale planting may also reveal plants that you did not know were there —winter-dormant herbaceous perennials, or spring, summer or autumn bulbs that suddenly spear through the bare earth. Always take care when digging in a new garden that has already been planted; you never know what wonderful treasures may be resting in the soil below. And do not be too hasty in doing away with dull-looking plants or shrubs, or plants that you do not recognise; they may surprise you later on.

It is always worth asking the previous owners for as much detail about the garden as possible. (What plants does it contain? Any 'special' plants? What is it like in summer, winter, etc.? Is its soil limy or acid, light and well drained or very sticky clay? Is it prone to severe frosts? Which spots get sun all year round, and which remain shady?) If you do not have an opportunity to quiz the previous owners, neighbours may be able to tell you quite a bit about it, and about their own gardens (which will often share the same conditions).

Improving the soil

I have already touched briefly on soil problems when discussing grass and shade, and I should now like to take a closer look at soil improvement generally, something that can really help you to make a success out of a small garden. Most of us are all too familiar with the kinds of soil which plague the owners of town gardens and plots on new housing estates: sticky clays, puddled and gooey all winter and baked hard as rock in summer; worn-out, dusty city soils; gardens full of builders' rubble or churned up by contractors' heavy machinery into a hotchpotch of good topsoil and lumpy, infertile subsoil.

The one thing that will improve all of these is humus, in the form of peat (as mentioned for lawns), spent mushroom compost, garden compost, well rotted manure, and so on. Even soils which seem to be in reasonable condition will still benefit from the addition of these materials, and if you are short of planting space then it makes sense to ensure that what ground you do have is going to give you the very best possible results.

Peat is an excellent soil-improving material, clean to handle and easily obtainable, although it does not put any plant foods into the ground as the others do; it needs to be enriched with compound fertiliser, if it is to help feed the plants as well as make dry soils more moisture-retentive and clay soils crumblier. Garden compost is the cheapest material, both good for the soil structure and full of plant nutrients, but in a tiny garden the problem is finding space for a heap. However, if you can make room for a plastic composting bin, which takes up less space than a traditional heap (and can be hidden behind a shrub), the garden will benefit in the long run.

In the tiniest of gardens even this may not be possible without the bin being an obtrusive feature. In this case there are still ways to make use of those grass clippings, and vegetable wastes from the kitchen such as cabbage leaves or potato peelings. Provided you follow some basic guidelines similar to those for compost heaps, these can be buried in the soil in bare patches between plants and shrubs. Spread the compost material around in various empty patches of soil, not too much in one spot; bury it in thin layers, covering each layer with a sprinkling of garden soil plus a large dose of compost accelerator or compound fertiliser, to help feed the bacteria necessary for decomposition (put a layer of compost material in

your hole, a layer of soil, a sprinkling of accelerator or fertiliser, more compost, and so on). And it is equally important to keep the underground compost away from the roots of nearby plants, so that the roots only grow into the compost after it is well rotted down.

In my first garden (the tiny courtyard) I tried this in desperation, unable to spare a corner for a compost heap, but unwilling to waste the clippings from my titchy lawn and the annual weeds which (if they are pulled out before they set seed) also make excellent compost. Provided these materials were buried a few inches away from roots, I found they did the plants no harm at all, and gave them a positive boost when they did eventually thrust their roots into the underground 'compost heaps'. There are always a few empty patches of ground between plants even in the most crowded garden, and particularly in the early days when many of the plants are still small; by working my way round these, burying compost 'treasure', I must have improved quite an area of soil.

An especially good time to do this is in late summer or autumn when plant growth is slowing down, so that you can bury compost materials even closer to the roots; by the following planting season, in spring or early summer, the rotted stuff can be mixed in with the soil ready for planting. But it works at any season, bearing in mind that the warmer the weather, the faster the roots spread and the further the compost should be buried from them.

I got the idea from organic vegetable growers who make great use of compost, frequently digging green plant material into the soil (known as 'green manuring') and lining the bottoms of bean and potato trenches with greenstuffs. If it was good enough for the spuds, I reasoned, then it was good enough for my shrubs and perennials.

Since then, I have often used fresh green composting materials when making entire new beds and borders, burying the stuff a good spade's depth below the surface, where the growing roots of small new plants can discover it, nicely rotted, a few months later.

I was taught early in my gardening life the value of burying turfs upside-down under the soil of new plant beds, if the beds were being cut out of a lawn, to rot down into a spongy layer; more sensible in a small garden than the usual recommendation to stack the stripped turf to rot down; and adding a few grass clippings and such like underneath the turfs seemed like a good idea. But even when renovating or replanting an existing bed (with no turfs to bury), a deeply-hidden layer of greenstuff will do almost as well on its own as a long-term soil conditioner.

I have even been known to make raised beds in this way for plants that love well-drained conditions (like my old favourites, the lilies); building up a pile of compost material in a hole in a spare corner, eventually covering it over with soil; planting three or four months later, once everything has settled nicely. The same rules apply in these cases: make sure that you bury the grass clippings or other rubbish well below the roots of plants that are to go in immediately.

Never bury perennial weed roots like dandelions or bindweed, or annual weeds which have formed seed pods; and do not use grass clippings if the lawn has recently been treated with weedkiller. Your 'underground compost' will, however, be the better for the addition of some coarser, tougher stuff like hedge clippings, autumn leaves or even shredded newspaper. But do not bury large amounts of these, because the soil bacteria use up a lot of the plant food nitrogen in rotting them down, and this can cause problems later on when your plants find the soil deficient in this essential nutrient. Always make sure that the compost bacteria will not rob the soil of nutrients by scattering on plenty of compound fertiliser (Blood, Fish and Bone is good) or a compost accelerator; and water the stuff well before covering it up, to speed decomposition.

Talking of burying things, another valuable early lesson I was taught was to get all soil-improving materials (peat, manure, compost or whatever) right down around the roots, and especially below them, when planting. This makes particular sense when you are working with the kinds of problem soils that I have already mentioned—the soils that owners of small gardens so often face. After all, if you are buying expensive peat, you will want to use it where it will do the most good, not spread thinly throughout the soil whether there are roots there or not. Complete and thorough enrichment of the entire bed or border is the ideal, but it is not always practical to do it all at once; in this case, the place to start is around individual plants.

If you do have a troublesome soil—a heavy clay for example—new plants will get off to a better start if the peat is dug into the base of the planting hole, with a little mixed into the soil to go around the roots, rather than spreading the peat too far and wide. This will help the roots to get established, and after that you will probably find the plant will look after itself even in poor soil. Even with established plants and shrubs, it is better to rake or gently fork the peat (or the compost) into the soil around and over the roots, rather than simply laying it as a mulch on the surface; but watch out for shallow-rooting plants like rhododendrons and conifers, where you need to go carefully and gently.

Using fertilisers

I am a strong believer in using organic or semi-organic mixes like John Innes Base (for mixing into the soil when planting) and Blood, Fish and Bone (for annual top-dressing); these are generally better for the soil in the long run than purely chemical-based fertilisers. Like compost, they encourage a healthy balance of essential soil bacteria working away to keep the ground fertile and help feed the plants; whereas too much non-organic fertiliser can upset the natural balance and produce a soil which is more 'dead' and reliant on more and more chemicals to keep it fertile. If you have only a small area of soil in which to grow things, you might as well treat it as kindly as possible, especially if the plants look better for it and give you a greater return per square metre.

The one chemical fertiliser that I could not do without, and which I would recommend to every owner of a small garden, is sulphate of potash. This is the best source of the plant nutrient potassium: essential for free flowering, rich flower colour, heavy cropping of fruits and pod vegetables, and for production of tough plant growth resistant to both disease and frost—a veritable plant cure-all. But, like most cure-alls, it must be used in moderation, as must all fertilisers unless you want to do more harm than good. A light sprinkling is all that is needed, in early spring, to give a boost to any plants or shrubs that do not seem to be flowering as well as they should.

Bulbs in particular seem to love potash, flowering better every year, ever larger, more colourful and more numerous. It seems to have an especially wonderful effect on those dwarf bulbs which otherwise make a habit of flowering for one year and then sulking or even disappearing, like the winter and spring flowering *Iris reticulata* varieties, the tiny hoop-petticoat *Narcissus bulbocodium* and other similar dainty beauties.

Plants which flower early in the year and tend to have their buds or blooms frost-damaged, like camellias and some early rhododendrons, also benefit from the frost-resistance and flowering boost that potash produces, as do any plants that are a little on the tender side and liable to suffer in severe winters.

I recommend annual top-dressings because potash is quickly washed away by heavy winter rains, particularly on fast-draining sandy, limy or chalky soils; and the garden can easily become deficient in this valuable nutrient. So whenever I am asked why such-and-such a plant in someone's garden does not flower as it used to (or has never started flowering at all) my usual answer is: 'try some potash'. In fact, try a little even on plants that you think are flowering quite well; you might be surprised at how much better they can do.

Raised beds

Apart from troublesome shade and difficult soils, one of the commonest problems in small gardens is the sheer flatness of the site, with no changes in level to add interest. Some gardeners face the opposite problem of too steep a slope for comfort, but at least in this case there is the opportunity to create a fascinating series of terraced beds with retaining walls (preferably with planting holes so that they can become beautiful wall gardens), and the outlook will be anything but boringly flat.

I have gardened both on completely level ground and on a steeply sloping valley side where the topsoil literally slid into the garden next door during heavy rainstorms. Without a doubt, a flat garden is the more difficult to make interesting (even if it is easier on the legs), but there is still a lot that can be done to add height and character.

As far as 'landscaping' goes, the best you can really hope to do in most small gardens is slightly to raise the level of one or two beds or borders, to create a more undulating ground-base on which to build extra height and interest, with varying sizes of evergreen shrubs and conifers, and perhaps a small tree. Even if you can only increase the height of a bed by 30 cm (12 ins), this will greatly help to break up the billiard-table look of a flat plot. Young evergreens planted towards the back of a raised bed will instantly appear slightly taller and more mature by virtue of their commanding position; and if you can arrange to have smaller plants to the fore, merging into the larger shrubs at the back, this will further increase the illusion of a steeply-rising bank.

A raised bed, because of its free-draining nature, also provides a perfect home for neat rock plants, dwarf conifers and miniature bulbs—all ideal plants for the tiny garden. It does not matter whether the bed is built up as a rock garden or simply as a gently sloping (or even flat) raised bed, with no rocks at all. The alpines, conifers and bulbs will love it either way; they like the sharp drainage, but the presence or absence of rocks makes little difference to them. A raised bed is also the ideal place to grow other plants that enjoy a well-drained position, like the lilies that I keep 'plugging'. These plants will be discussed more fully in later chapters.

How exactly can you raise the level of beds and borders in a small garden, without buying in a lorry-load of extra soil, or bags and bags of peat and mushroom compost?

The ideal answer would be exactly that: to import additional material for building up the level of the beds. But, apart from the expense,

Even very low raised beds add interest to a garden ; slow-growing conifers with Daphne retusa, Hypericum olympicum *and the handsome foliage of* Paeonia mlokosewitschii.

access to many of the smallest town and city gardens (e.g. in terraces, mews, etc.) is through the house or via narrow passageways, making delivery of bulky garden materials difficult.

Some peat or other humus-adding stuff might be used, with the dual purpose of raising the bed level and improving the soil. But the height of the bed may also be increased by first excavating it and dumping any old, useless materials into the base—old bricks, broken paving slabs, stones, the detritus from house renovations; in fact, almost anything at all that you want to get rid of. This kind of rubble or rubbish will actually improve the drainage, making the beds even more suitable for alpines. And even larger perennials and shrubs will not mind, provided there is a reasonable layer of soil on top and they are given some peat to help them get started.

On top of this, you can lay composting materials as previously suggested—annual weeds, grass and hedge clippings, kitchen vegetable waste, up-turned turfs and so on—finally replacing the soil, preferably improved and enriched with humus materials and fertiliser. For rock plants, the soil is best made even more free-draining with extra grit or sharp sand.

The raising of planting beds and borders can be accentuated if a path or paved area running alongside or through them is excavated to a slightly lower level. This increases the 'landscaping' effect twofold: the path or paving level drops, while the bed rises, so that the soil level seems even higher than it really is in relation to the average garden level. This may sound like hard work, but the excavation of the non-planting area need not be very deep before the effect starts to become obvious, and even just 15–20 cm (6–8 ins) will make a difference. In this way, you are also making use of the good topsoil that would otherwise disappear beneath the gravel or paving; better to use the soil, and lay the path or paved area on useless subsoil (with a bedding of sand for slabs, of course.)

If you are planning a paved area, this will probably be the central feature, with the beds rising all around. With a sunken path running between raised beds or borders, the best plan is gradually to dip the path lower and lower towards the centre, then slowly let it rise back to normal level at the other end; alternatively, the shelving path could lead down to a small paved or grassed area (perhaps as a sitting-out area), or it could return to garden level at the other end via a couple of steps. However, beware of making this kind of sunken path or paved area too deep if your soil is very heavy and prone to waterlogging in winter; otherwise you may find the lowest sections flooding after heavy rains. Putting down some hardcore or rubble below the gravel or paving slabs in the lowest sections may help in this situation.

A winding path like this, gently meandering through raised beds, would make an attractive feature in any garden and, with a small paved section for sitting and relaxing, would provide an interesting layout for a tiny courtyard garden if there were really insufficient space for both a lawn and decent-sized borders. Depending on how much you raised the bed levels, you might need to build a low retaining wall or two, to hold back the soil. These can be highly decorative features, whether made of stone, brick or reconstructed stone blocks. Retaining walls also make useful seats from which to admire, plant and weed.

If you are building retaining walls, always leave plenty of holes so that plants can be inserted, with their roots delving into the soil behind, to create yet another delightful feature. Once again, a wall garden of this sort is the ideal place for rock plants; particularly trailers, like the aubrietas, *Campanula garganica*, and *Phlox subulata*, which will cascade downwards in a sheet of bright colour; or alpines that enjoy a really sheltered and dry position, like the lewisias. And on north-facing retaining wall gardens, beautiful shade-loving plants like ferns, primroses and the autumn-flowering *Gentiana sino-ornata* will thrive.

Whether the wall is to be laid dry or cemented, it is generally best to plant as you build, so that the roots may be carefully spread back into the soil. This is much more satisfactory than trying to cram the roots into the holes later on.

When you think about it, this kind of retaining wall garden actually increases the available planting room in a small garden quite appreciably (for example, a wall 45 cm (18 ins) high and 3 m (10 ft) long comes to a total additional area of nearly 1.5 sq m (15 sq ft) over which your wall plants can spread). And such walls need not be very tall; even one just 30 cm (1 ft) high and with plenty of planting holes, edging a bed or border, will accommodate a fair number of plants. But if you can go higher, so much the better. Retaining walls without planting holes can be almost as useful; trailing plants can still utilise the extra growing space, cascading down from the top of the wall and spreading into large plants without taking up valuable room in the ground behind.

Should you decide to raise the level of a bed without retaining walls, it is essential to ensure that the bed slopes *gradually* upwards towards the back; otherwise, if the slope is too steep, the soil will be continually washing down onto the path or the lawn, leaving plants towards the front with their roots exposed. And should you decide that it is impossible to play around with the soil levels, and that the garden will have to stay rather flat, then concentrate on creating your variations in height and scale with the plants themselves. Bear in mind what I said about building your shrubs and plants up in a 'banked' effect, the tallest towards the back of the border (or in a corner, or towards the end of the garden) and the smaller plants to the fore; with the occasional tall specimen plant or shrub rising up amongst the shorter plants for contrast.

These are, of course, very general suggestions; it is up to the individual to work out his or her detailed planting plans according to taste and inspiration.

Island beds

Any discussion of beds and borders leads to the question of the 'island' bed. I do not think that this plays as great a role in very small gardens as it does elsewhere. If space is restricted, the lawn may be so small that it would be difficult to cut out a decent-sized island bed without virtually slicing the lawn in half and spoiling it; and the alternative would be a minuscule circular hole in which only a few plants could be grown—a mean-looking little feature barely worth having. In this case, I should say, do without a bed in the lawn and enjoy an uninterrupted expanse of grass while making the most of the borders.

If you do have space for a bed in the grass, and if it can only be a small one, then my suggestion would be to use it as a planting site for a small tree or a medium-sized shrub or conifer (ideally with some small bulbs for spring or autumn planted around its feet). Planting with herbaceous perennials or bedding plants is far from satisfactory on a small scale; during the cold months you are faced with a bare patch of soil sitting miserably in the middle of the lawn and crying out for something more permanent and distinctive like a handsome evergreen. After all, if you have room for an island bed, then this should be a focal point, a place of honour in which to show off something spectacular and worthy of an isolated position; something like your one and only tree, perhaps, a rhododendron or some other evergreen shrub with a touch of class.

Covering walls and ugly features

Hiding ugly features or views is often a priority in a small garden, but this can also be an excuse for some imaginative and exciting planting. Take, for example, that old problem the manhole cover, slap bang in the middle of the garden; there is any number of ground-covering plants which, tucked around the edges, will quickly disguise it. But for solid year-round camouflage, use something evergreen, dense and widely spreading like a prostrate conifer (a fast-growing *Juniperus horizontalis* variety, or *J. procumbens* 'Nana'). Add a couple of heathers (the winter-flowering *Erica carnea* varieties if your soil is limy), a small upright conifer like *Chamaecyparis lawsoniana* 'Ellwoodii' or the conical *Picea glauca albertiana* 'Conica', and you have an instant feature that will provide interest throughout the year.

Low-growing evergreen plants are also useful alongside paths and paving, to soften the harsh edges; but if the path is in regular use, do not plant anything too strong (such as a fast-growing, spreading conifer) which may need regular cutting back; go for neater plants like the heathers, helianthemums, *Cotoneaster congestus*, thymes or *Hypericum olympicum*. Further examples of ground-covering plants can be found in Chapter Five.

Larger problems—unsightly outbuildings, ugly garages, rickety fences or tumbledown walls —call for strong-growing climbers: honeysuckles, vigorous clematis species like *C. montana*, vines, etc.

Quite apart from their usefulness in brightening up bare walls and fences and improving unattractive buildings, climbing plants give the gardener fantastic value in return for a tiny planting space. They should certainly be used more in small gardens, if only for these two reasons. I love climbers for the sheer luxuriance of growth and flower that they can bring into the most confined of spaces, softening the hard lines of walls and fences and producing a show to rival any tree or large shrub; yet without casting unwanted shade (like a tree) or spreading across yards of valuable soil (like many large shrubs).

I also like them because they fit so well into the casual or cottage-garden style of planting that I find suits today's tiny gardens so admirably; just as they did in the old cottage gardens, climbers rambling over house walls and up into trees add a romantic touch of 'wildness' and lush abandon to the scene (provided they are allowed to spread a little and are not treated to an annual poodletrim). Probably the most attractive choices where space is limited are those that offer the additional delight of summer fragrance, like the ever-popular honeysuckles and white jasmine.

Much of the blame for the fact that beautiful climbers are not seen more in small gardens lies, I am sure, with the concrete paths that surround so many modern houses, often without so much as a narrow border between path and house wall.

Builders should realise what a boon beds against sunny house walls are to the keen gardener. Such warm spots provide sheltered havens for all kinds of semi-hardy things and plants that only flower well if they get a hot summer baking. But, most importantly, they allow climbers to be planted, to clothe the walls with fresh greenery and sheets of colour. If you have this problem, and you yearn for honeysuckle round the door and the sweet scent of jasmine wafting through the windows on warm summer evenings, there are two things you can do: you can either grow your climbers in tubs or, like me, take a hammer

and chisel to the concrete and make some small planting holes.

The latter suggestion may sound like hard work, but I have found it highly rewarding. Most concrete paths are quite thinly laid over hardcore and sand; breaking through takes a little patience, but once you have made a small hole, enlarging it is no problem. Scoop out the rocks and sand, fill in with some potting compost, and you have a snug little planting site all ready for that climber you have always wanted by the front door, the kitchen window, or wherever. The roots will spread happily through the cool soil beneath the concrete, requiring watering only in the hottest spells (although regular watering is best in the first year, to encourage rapid establishment). Feeding is probably best done with liquid fertiliser in spring and summer, so that the plant foods are washed well under the concrete to the furthest extremes of the roots.

Some visitors to my garden, on seeing climbers planted in this way, worry about possible damage to the foundations from roots; and I often find myself answering letters from gardeners concerned about shrubs and climbers on their own house walls. I have never come across a case of this sort of damage resulting from putting climbing plants and shrubs against walls, and gardeners have been doing this for centuries. However, strong-rooting trees like poplars and large willows can of course cause damage to walls. The risk of damage is highest where the soil is a heavy clay which will shrink when the tree roots dry it out fast in summer, possibly leading to subsidence problems. Few climbers or shrubs could do this to anything like the same extent, but where the soil is a heavy clay, it is probably better to avoid planting the very strongest and largest climbers and shrubs against the house walls, just to be on the safe side, and particularly if the house (or its neighbours) already has a history of subsidence trouble. Having said that, I must emphasise that most of the climbers normally used on house walls (clematis, honeysuckle, jasmine, roses, etc.) usually cause no serious problems.

Hydrangea petiolaris, Polygonum baldschuanicum and *P. aubertii* are some of the most rampant climbers of all. Even these are frequently seen happily romping over house walls with no sign of any serious damage, but they can get out of hand in a confined space. They are superb for covering a tall wall or smothering an outbuilding in no time at all, and are probably the fastest-growing climbers commonly available. But they can become a nuisance: they bush out from the wall and may need frequent trimming if they are not to block paths. And once they get a hold, they will cover everything in sight, including windows which will need to be kept cleared, and any neighbouring climbers and shrubs. So beware these unless you really do have a large wall or building which you want to cover very quickly; otherwise, go for less rampant climbers which are not quite so space-hungry and which will not try to strangle nearby plants to death. I would rather have a variety of climbers than an overpowering mass of just one thing, as, I expect, would most gardeners.

Apart from the true climbers, there are many shrubs which, when planted at the base of a wall or fence, will push their way upwards to provide an attractive covering—the bright-berried pyracanthas, for example. But do not forget that many of these wall shrubs are, by their nature, large and vigorous things, and they tend to bush out from the wall as well as climb skywards. Where they become a nuisance (for example, beside a path) this may mean that hard regular pruning will eventually be called for, which in turn may mean few flowers or berries. If there is little room for something that is going to become at all bushy, stick to true climbers whose growth can generally be more easily trained upwards and out of the way.

Structural planting: trees, shrubs and hedges
Having mentioned climbers that can get out of hand, I should like to take a quick look at choosing trees and shrubs for small gardens. There are quite a few trees suitable for restricted spaces, although most of these can, in time, reach a fair size. You may be put off by reading in gardening books that an eventual height of 4.5–6 m (15–20 ft) and a spread of 3–4.5 m (10–15 ft) is not unusual for even small trees like the mountain ash, flowering crab apples and the colourful

flowering hawthorns; and that many of the popular flowering cherries can grow larger still. However, it may well take these trees 20 years or more to attain such dimensions, and even the fastest growers among them can be relied upon to stay under 4.5 m (15 ft) for at least the first ten years. So the message certainly is not 'do not plant trees', but quite the opposite: do not be afraid to plant a tree, no matter how small the garden; but the tinier your growing space, the greater the care you should take over selection. Even though flowering cherries, mountain ash, hawthorn, acers, crab apples and such like are commonly recommended for small gardens, remember that within these general groups there are larger trees and smaller varieties; if you are tight for space, search out the latter types.

For the most compact gardens, there are a few very slow-growing trees which always remain truly tiny, like *Acer palmatum*, one of the loveliest of the Japanese maples; or *Acer griseum*, the handsome paperbark maple. And there are also one or two small trees which take on an upright, columnar shape instead of spreading, like the flowering cherry 'Amanogawa'.

Where there is a little more space, but still room for only one tree, or maybe two, I think my first choice would always be one of the smaller cherries, even if the spring blossom is rather fleeting; most have such handsome trunks and symmetrically pleasing habits, while the spring and autumn leaves often colour well. Since I shall be discussing small trees in Chapter Four, all I shall say here is that if you can possibly fit a tree into the garden, then do. Trees, even small ones, add so much character; and to me a garden without one always seems bare.

The alternative is to make do with a large shrub or two which can be relied upon to reach 3 m (10 ft) or so, spreading out nicely at the top like a small tree. Some of the taller cotoneasters, for example, although strictly speaking shrubs, do make handsome small trees. *Genista aetnensis* (the Mount Etna broom) is another, and so is the popular *Magnolia soulangeana*. It is also possible to prune the lower branches of some large shrubs, to give them a clean trunk and more of a tree shape.

Speaking of large shrubs, do not forget that many are definitely oversized for the small garden, even if they do look neat in the garden centre. And remember that it is not just height you need to know about; how much a shrub spreads is equally important, if not more so. Many grow as much in diameter as in height, and some sprawl more sideways than upwards.

If you are not sure, always ask about ultimate size (and speed and habit of growth) when buying; or, better still, check for yourself in a reliable reference book such as *The Hillier Colour Dictionary of Trees and Shrubs* or the *Reader's Digest Encyclopaedia of Garden Plants and Flowers* (which, very handily, gives estimates of spread as well as height). In particular, beware of large suckering shrubs, like the all too popular stag's horn sumach, *Rhus typhina*, which pushes up its unwanted suckers all over the place and can become a real pest.

The same comments go for conifers, particularly the fastest-growing types recommended for hedging. Bear in mind that *Cupressocyparis leylandii* (probably now the most popular of all hedging plants) can reach 15 m (50 ft) in good soil, and 9 m (30 ft) or more even on shallow soils; it can also spread at the base to as much as 3 m (10 ft) in diameter. Even some of the 'slower-growing' hedging conifers like *Chamaecyparis lawsoniana* can reach almost the same dimensions in time (unless you deliberately pick the smaller forms, which are much slower). As hedges around a small garden, these fast conifers will have to be stopped (the tops taken out) as soon as they reach the desired height, and after that they will require heavy annual pruning to keep them neat. Leave them too long and you could have a real problem on your hands. It always seems a shame to me that these majestic conifers (so handsome when grown as the trees that they are, but requiring more space than most small gardens have to spare) have to be pruned and trimmed into neat hedges to fit the available space.

When treated like this, they are not much more attractive than boring old privet, and to my eye they actually look worse. We can accept privet, beech, thorn, yew, etc., as trimmed hedges because we are used to them as traditional hedging materials. But conifers are comparatively new to gardens, introduced for their lovely evergreen shapeliness and variety of foliage colour. To see them as manicured hedges is an even newer experience in the British street scene, and I for one do not like it. The trouble is, I think, that most hedging conifers produce their foliage in large fan-shaped branchlets which look stubby and ugly when cut back, just as laurels never look quite right when neatly trimmed with their large leaves cut in half. And I can almost see those elegant pointed peaks which ought to be swaying in the breeze, but which have had to be hacked down to stumps.

In any case, there are plenty of other hedging plants to choose from, many far more interesting than trimmed conifers. I personally like beech for its fresh green spring leaves, turning darker as summer progresses and finally taking on warm autumn tints of coppery-russet which last until the buds burst again in spring; how many evergreens can provide that sort of colour-change and interest throughout the year? And yet beech is as good as evergreen, holding its autumn leaves right through the winter. Beech is a little slow to get started, but then so is the triffid-like leylandii, which will often put on little growth in its first season or two; give beech a chance, and it will soon be growing 45 cm (18 ins) a year.

Should you decide to use conifers for hedging, do consider something comparatively slow-growing which will not have to be hacked about, and which will therefore retain its natural beauty of form; at least to some extent.

Conifers are of course equally popular as garden trees, and they make very attractive evergreen features, either as single specimens or in groups of contrasting shape and colour. But here again, care should be taken in selecting truly slow-growing trees for those restricted spaces in the garden. Since conifers came into vogue, many gardeners have found that, over the years, what they thought would be neat little dwarfs have turned out to be monsters in disguise; and many

Conifers and broad-leaved shrubs contrast well in this corner. The neat shrubs to the right are the fragrant spring-flowering Daphne retusa.

29

is the tale I have heard of 'miniature' conifers eventually taking over rock gardens and blocking paths and windows. This does not happen overnight, but it is amazing what a small conifer can do over a period of years. Once again, the answer is thoroughly to check on growth rates.

When you are buying (or looking at trees in other gardens), see how long the new green shoots are, bearing in mind the time of year; any conifer which has produced new growth of more than 5 or 8 cm (2 or 3 ins) in a year is not really suitable for a very small rock garden, and anything that has new shoots more than 15 cm (6 ins) in length will become quite large in time.

Remember also that the conifers may be growing slowly in the nursery because they are pot-bound and short of water; in garden soil they may rocket upwards much faster. And do not forget that, like shrubs, conifers can spread sideways a fair distance, taking up more room every year as well as reaching for the sky; this applies particularly to the bushy and conical varieties which broaden excessively at the base and may eventually take up a square metre of soil or more.

The same rule-of-thumb test (checking length of annual growth) can also be applied to shrubs and trees, particularly when buying during the autumn planting season, when annual growth is complete (although the speed and length of new spring growth gives almost as good an indication). This is a more reliable guide than an off-hand guess from a harassed garden centre assistant on a busy Easter weekend. Simply estimate the new growth and multiply by a few years to get an idea of height; and look for bushy or narrowly-upright habit, combined with speed of growth, to estimate spread.

Even when choosing non-shrubby perennial plants, it is worth checking on eventual size and spread, since many can become fairly big as they mature; some grow so large and leafy that the flowering display does not really warrant the space they take up in a small garden. It is generally better to have two neat plants, for variety and different flowering periods, than one sprawling giant. The exceptions are those plants which, although on the large side, flower over a very long period, or which provide additional interesting features as discussed earlier.

A quart into a pint pot

Apart from trying to concentrate on neat-growing plants and shrubs, there are plenty of space-saving ideas which can help the keen gardener to squeeze as much as possible into the smallest spaces. The most obvious (and I do not think that this can be repeated too often) is adopting an informal mixed, or cottage-garden style of planting where the ideal is to end up with hardly a centimetre of bare soil in sight; plants and shrubs blending into and rambling through one another in a riot of foliage and flower.

But it is not simply a matter of putting the plants close together, to get almost total ground-cover. Even within this apparently simple and casual approach, it is possible to come up with additional ideas and refinements to help make maximum use of the available ground.

Climbers in abundance

Climbers, as I have said, are great space-savers; but they need not be confined to walls and fences alone. They can be trained up into trees so that, for example, the early spring blossom of a small cherry might be followed by the flowers of a clematis scrambling up the trunk, cascading down from the tree's branches and peeping out from amongst the foliage. Honeysuckles can be used in the same way, as can many other climbing plants. The climber can either be trained right up into the branches, or it can use just the trunk for support, being trimmed down annually; personally, I usually prefer to let climbers 'do their thing', without too much pruning, to get a more natural look.

Climbers can also be planted beneath large shrubs, to twine their way upwards and burst out from the topmost foliage in a blaze of colour when the shrub is out of flower—two seasons of colour from one space. But do ensure that they bloom at different times, otherwise the effect will be spoilt and you will find yourself with an odd mixture of blooms and still only the one flowering period. This is a particularly easy way to liven up a clump of laurels or other boring shrubs that you might have inherited in a new garden. Even a hedge can be given a new look with a climber scrambling through it (although you will have to take a little care over hedge trimming and avoid damaging the climber's shoots before the flowers have finished).

The one thing to bear in mind is that the plant chosen for the climber to grow through must be thoroughly established and large enough to stand the competition; a recently planted or very small shrub or tree could be strangled. If the climber gets out of hand, it may need regular cutting back. When planting a climber in this situation, take care not to damage the shrub or tree roots too much; place the climber a little way out from the trunk, where it will also get more rainwater than in the dry soil right under the branches. Prepare the planting site well, with plenty of peat or compost; and keep both the tree (or shrub) and the climber well fed and watered for the first year or two, since they will be competing for water and nutrients; forget this, and they could both suffer.

Remember also my advice regarding walls with concrete paths or patios at the base: do not waste the wall space; plant climbers in tubs or make holes in the concrete (or lift a flagstone if the area is paved). You do not need a sunny wall to grow climbers and wall shrubs. Quite a number will survive on shady walls or fences—*Jasminum officinale*, ivies, honeysuckles, *Clematis montana*, Virginia creeper, and the rampant *Polygonum baldschuanicum*, *P. aubertii* and *Hydrangea petiolaris*, to name just a few.

Thorough soil preparation is especially important for climbers grown against walls and fences. The soil here is often sheltered even from heavy rain, becoming very dry in spring and summer. It may also be full of builders' sand and rubble. Place the plant at least 20 cm (8 ins) out from the wall, where more rain will reach its roots, and give it plenty of soil-improving materials to retain summer moisture.

There is no need to confine yourself to one climber per wall; if you are very short of growing room, it would be a shame to waste valuable wall or fence space on just one plant, particularly since wall plants give such good value for such a little soil room. Try planting a couple of climbers or wall shrubs (or more) for colour at different seasons, even if the wall or fence is quite small.

For example, you might try an early-flowering species clematis like *C. montana* and a late-flowering one like the yellow *C. tangutica* or *C. orientalis*, or a later-flowering hybrid, perhaps. Or you might fancy the yellow winter-flowering *Jasminum nudiflorum* with the summer-blooming *J. officinale* scrambling up through it; an early clematis with *Lonicera japonica* to carry on the display through summer; a rose for summer and a vine or creeper for autumn leaf tints; or any permutation you care to think up.

If the climbers intermingle and grow into one another (or even grow up one another, completely intertwined, having been planted close together), what is wrong with that? It may make subsequent pruning a little more awkward, but the effect and the extra colour and interest will be worth the trouble.

Plants under plants

Underplanting is another excellent way to pack extra plants into the garden, making use of the soil under trees and shrubs for low-growing or 'carpeting' plants and bulbs, rather than leaving the ground bare. Any shrub can be underplanted, even the rose bushes which many enthusiasts believe should be grown on their own with nothing but bare soil beneath. That rule only applies if you are trying to grow oversized prize-winning roses for the show bench; in the average small garden we are generally after masses of flowers, not a few football-sized blooms, and the odd plant for extra colour around the feet of the roses will do no harm at all.

Where you have a tree or a shrub which branches high up, so that the ground below is completely naked, any gardener will quickly spot the desirability of covering this bare patch with plants that will not mind the dry soil (and perhaps shade) of such a situation. But I like to take underplanting further than this, finding room for a few plants even under shrubs which have branches right down to ground level.

Small early spring bulbs, like crocus, snowdrops, eranthis, scillas and chionodoxas can be planted under deciduous shrubs even if the lower branches actually lie on the soil; the little bulbs will pop up while the branches are bare in late winter and early spring, disappearing below ground again as the new foliage expands on the shrub. And lilies can be planted to spear up through low shrubs (whether deciduous or evergreen) in summer.

Where you have large shrubs with branches and foliage to the ground, taking up a lot of space in a small garden, it is an even better idea to remove some of the lower branches to free the soil for a wider range of underplanting. After all, shrubs can quickly gobble up a lot more room than the gardener intended; and if there is a way to grab back some of that valuable growing space, while retaining the shrubs, it should certainly be considered. You might feel that lopping some of the lower branches is unnatural and will make the shrub look 'leggy', but if it is done carefully it can look good, particularly once you have established some lovely plants to fill the gap around the trunk.

There is in fact no reason why a shrub *should* have foliage and branches right down to ground level, unless it is actually intended as solid ground-cover over a patch of very poor soil which will grow nothing else (and even then, why not improve the soil if planting room is valuable?). Gardeners already prune and train many trees, and some shrubs, too, as standards with clean trunks. And in the wild, shrubs and trees usually drop their lower limbs quite naturally as they grow upwards towards the light, in competition with surrounding plants, shrubs and trees, ending up with bare trunks towards the base. It is often only the artificial, orderly and less crowded conditions of garden life that permit shrubs to get enough sunlight and freedom from competition to allow them the luxury of retaining foliage right to the ground.

You could easily argue, therefore, that trimming a few lower branches and thus clearing the ground below for planting is as 'natural' as anything else. You are only doing what nature, given a chance, would probably do anyway. That is what we do with a tree when we remove branches and train the leading shoot to produce the sort of clean trunk that is normally seen in a wood, and that we like to see in the garden. If it is all right for

trees and some shrubs, then why not for all shrubs?

Naturally, I am not suggesting that everyone should go out and do this with every shrub in the garden; there may well be lovely shrubs that you do not want to touch. But it is a useful idea that can come in very handy when planting room is at a premium, especially where very straggly and space-hungry shrubs are concerned.

I mentioned earlier tall shrubs which take on a tree-like appearance, making them useful alternatives to full-sized trees for tight situations; in this case cleaning up the trunk completely, removing all lower branches, is a good idea if you want to emphasise the tree shape.

With most shrubs, particularly those that are bushy and rounded, or low and spreading in shape, rather than tall and thin, it is best to remove only the minimum number of lower branches necessary to allow for underplanting (and for the plants to be seen and admired). Do this carefully, sawing the branches off as close to the trunk as possible, to give a clean and natural effect (leaving a short stump is unnecessary; the branches can be sawn off almost flush with the trunk and the cuts will heal over perfectly well).

Another planting site that is frequently overlooked is along the bottoms of hedges. No one would want to trim away all the lower branches of a hedge to make more planting room, thereby spoiling the screening effect; but most mature hedges are a little bare at the base anyway, even when the gardener has made a conscious attempt to keep them bushy, and there is often room for a few neat plants or bulbs along the hedge bottom —perhaps 'wild' plants like violets, primroses, wood anemones or snowdrops to create a little 'hedgerow garden'; bulbs for a colourful spring display, or strong-growing autumn bulbs like the large-flowered colchicums.

Obviously, anything you plant beneath a tree or shrub (or along a hedge bottom) must be suited to the situation. It is no use expecting a large, leafy and water-hungry border plant to thrive in the dry soil under overhanging branches and amongst tough roots. Nor can you expect a sun-loving plant to enjoy being under a shrub if that means it will be in shade. Should the shrub be in

Screening the view ahead can create illusions of space. Here a home-made trough on the path contains a dwarf box tree with small, colourful plants trailing round it : Hypericum olympicum, Campanula fenestrellata *and the small* Mimulus *hybrid 'Whitecroft Scarlet'*. Primula sikkimensis *towers behind.*

Masking boundaries. Above: Placing larger shrubs at the rear of the border, grading down to smaller subjects at the front, will give an attractive 'banked' effect ; better still if a slight slope can also be created. This collection includes philadelphus, hypericums and potentillas. Left : A trellis billows with the old rose 'Madame Alfred Carrière', mingling with the blowsy, blue-flowering Clematis *'Mrs Cholmondeley'.*

Soften hard edges with plants that spread and tumble. Above: Concrete steps made beautiful with blue and white forms of Campanula carpatica *interplanted with the yellow* Hypericum olympicum.

Right: A path bordered by evergreen cistus and helianthemum, with the long-flowering Geranium endressii *'Wargave Pink' rambling through them.*

Stunning effects can be achieved quite simply. Here Campanula persicifolia *and* Hemerocallis *'Golden Chimes' create a beautiful display set off by dark shrubs. Both flower throughout the summer.*

an open position, however, the soil beneath could just as easily be sunny and dry, with little shade at all. And where the branches come low to the ground, you will in any case want only neat carpeting plants.

Small spring bulbs are an obvious choice, providing useful early colour and being undeterred by summer drought—in fact, they enjoy it. The same goes for autumn bulbs like the colchicums, the blue-flowered *Crocus speciosus* and the hardy cyclamen (particularly the pink-flowered and silver-leaved *Cyclamen neapolitanum*, now correctly known as *C. hederifolium*).

Lilies, as I have mentioned, enjoy sprouting up through low shrubs or leaning out from under larger ones; the branches and shrub roots help to keep their bulbs dry in winter (which they like) and they appreciate some shade over their roots, to keep them cool in summer. The one thing to watch with the lilies is that they do not get too dry in spring and early summer when they are pushing up their flowering spikes. They will also benefit from regular feeding and mulches of peat or compost, since they are in competition with the shrub roots.

Primroses and polyanthus are good in shady spots under shrubs and trees, but if they get too much sun they will suffer during summer. Small ferns, such as the dainty maidenhair-like *Adiantum pedatum*, also do well in shade. *Anemone nemorosa* (the wood anemone) and its blue-flowered varieties enjoy similar situations, as do the low-growing evergreen or semi-evergreen epimediums, the popular large-leaved hostas and some violets. The winter and spring flowering hellebores (the Lenten roses, Christmas roses, etc.) are happy under shrubs and trees, whether in shade or sun.

Where the soil beneath the shrub gets a fair amount of sun, you could try any low-growing and drought-resistant plants: dwarf geraniums (for example, the pink *G. sanguineum*), heathers, dianthus, helianthemums, strong dwarf campanulas like *C. carpatica*, small ornamental grasses, *Viola cornuta*, the evergreen bergenias, aubrietas and tuberous anemones.

Under trees and the tallest shrubs, where there is more headroom but equally dry soil, you can even plant small, tough ground-covering shrubs like potentillas, dwarf brooms and berberis, hebes, and hypericums. Provided the shade is not dense and they get some light, these low-growing shrubs will do very well; they may become a little more straggly than usual, but an occasional trim with the shears will put that right.

Bearing in mind the dryness of the soil under trees and shrubs (particularly in full sun) and the competition from the roots, any help you can give plants in these situations is well worthwhile. Generally improving the soil and building up its depth with peat, compost, etc., is the ideal answer; but even just a little peat and fertiliser in each planting hole will help the plants to get going, as will attention to watering and liquid feeding in the first season.

In future years, be sure to top-dress from time to time with a compound fertiliser like John Innes Base or Blood, Fish and Bone, because the soil has to feed both the shrubs (or trees) and the plants beneath, and it may quickly become exhausted. Mulching occasionally with peat or compost will also help to keep the soil in good condition and the plants happy. But then, the tougher and more suitable the plants you choose, the less you will need to worry about them.

Packing beds and borders

Space-saving underplanting need not be restricted to tucking a few extra plants under the shrubs and trees. If, like me, you are very short of growing room, then you will find, as you try to cram in as many plants as possible, that underplanting of a sort spreads even into the open areas of the beds and borders.

Many gardeners have discovered that plants enjoy 'root-association'—where they are grown close enough together for their roots as well as their foliage to intermingle—and I have always found this to be true with most of the plants that I have grown. It seems to be particularly true on heavy and poorly drained soils which are prone to waterlogging in winter. Where the ground is crammed full with the intertwining roots of different plants growing close together, this helps to keep the soil 'open' and in good condition; whereas an isolated plant with empty and badly drained ground around its root ball will be more prone to root rot and failure.

In addition, various beneficial fungi and bacteria live around plant roots, helping to feed the plants by gathering and breaking down chemical and organic materials in the ground into plant foods. (This is one of the major reasons for using plenty of compost and organic fertilisers on the garden; such organic materials feed the friendly micro-organisms which in turn feed the plant roots.) It seems highly likely that these useful bacteria and fungi can more easily spread from one plant to another when the roots are growing in an interconnecting mass, thereby maintaining a better general balance of soil fertility and ensuring that new plants and any which, for whatever reasons, lack a good complement of micro-organisms around their roots, soon acquire fresh supplies. It is worth remembering that over-heavy doses of purely chemical fertilisers, like sulphate of ammonia, can destroy these beneficial micro-organisms in the soil, or at least upset the natural balance.

When plants are crammed closely together, the dense ground-covering effect of the foliage may also be beneficial. Some people would say that the more plants there are per square metre, the more water is drawn up by the roots and evaporated away from the leaves during dry summer weather. But no one, to my knowledge, has carried out controlled scientific tests to work out which has more effect: the extra water loss through massed foliage, or the sheltering effect of ground-covering leaves keeping the soil and roots shaded and cool, and helping to trap moist air below, so that water evaporation direct from the soil is reduced.

From observing my own closely-packed plants, I should think that, to some extent, the two probably balance out. It also seems logical that a dense cover of foliage prevents heavy rain from compacting the surface of the soil, thereby keeping it more open and well aerated.

I mention the above points in an attempt to show that really cramming things into the garden, and creating almost total ground-cover in a cottage tangle of plants, should not create too many problems, and that the plants do actually enjoy it—always provided that you take care not to plant very strong and rampant things too close to smaller plants, and that you keep an eye open for any over-ambitious plants that start to cover up or throttle their neighbours.

With all this in mind, I have never thought twice about putting plants virtually shoulder-to-shoulder and allowing them to 'join hands'. And I have seldom had any problems with my practice of putting neat carpeting plants around the crowns of taller perennials, so that the low-growing plants can spread happily under the dappled shade of the loftier plants' foliage.

This is in fact a good way to grow small plants which appreciate a little summer shade, like primroses and various primulas. It is a particularly useful scheme to plant small spring-flowering subjects like these around the base of a tall perennial which blooms a little later; like early primroses or pulsatillas under a paeony, or early summer-flowering primulas tucked around the base of a clump of later-flowering crocosmias, and so on. When the early display is over, the larger plant will be shooting up to take over.

The only point to watch is that you do not put small sun-loving plants (particularly rock plants) too close to something taller which produces very large and floppy leaves that will totally cover the tinier neighbour. You will no doubt discover your own selection of tall perennials which can be 'underplanted' with smaller subjects; but they should be plants which produce tall, strong shoots with the leaves reasonably high up off the ground, or plants with upright sword-like leaves which only flop over late in the year.

Amongst the tall plants that I find ideal are the single-flowered paeony species and hybrids, irises, crocosmias, tall campanulas like *C. persicifolia*, schizostylis, hemerocallis, eremurus, gladioli, hardy fuchsias, Japanese anemones and lilies. These are all comparatively un-floppy and upright-growing perennials, under and round which it is fairly safe to put close plantings of smaller things.

It is, of course, an old herbaceous border trick

Part of the author's small rock garden in May ; an example of successful close planting.

to put early-flowering plants very close to later-flowering subjects that will fill the space after the early flowers are over, the larger and later summer plants often being allowed to flop partially over onto the spring plants. And it is even more useful in the mixed borders of the small garden, so long as you ensure that any plants being partially covered will not object—they should like a little shade anyway, or they should be tough, spreading plants that can cope with a little competition. Naturally, the early plants do not have to be smaller underplantings; large plants for early summer colour, for example, can be mixed in with large plants for a later display, all happily intermingling.

Bulbs, bulbs everywhere
Apart from utilising the soil under and around tall perennials, it is a good idea to consider bulb planting in the beds and borders as yet another 'layer' in the underplanting scheme. A well-stocked small garden will inevitably be planted in layers—a tree or two, then shrubs, then perennials under and between the shrubs, low-growing perennials around and under the taller plants, and finally bulbs under them all.

Spring and autumn bulbs have already been mentioned as perfect underplantings for shrubs and trees, along with other suitable small plants; and this is the best place for many of them, particularly the smaller types. They all take a summer rest, of course, and during this time they prefer the soil to be decidedly on the dry side, so the conditions under shrubs and trees (and hedges) suit them well. And many of the tiniest bulbs look very good amongst rock plants in raised beds or in rock gardens, where once again the well-drained soil will help to keep them from getting too wet in summer; here the strongest-growing varieties can be underplanted beneath trailing or carpeting plants, although any 'special' bulbs, rarities or particular favourites are best with little pockets of the rock garden or raised bed to themselves.

Spring bulbs in ordinary beds and borders can leave dreadful gaps during the summer, and I am often asked by owners of small gardens what they can do about this. The question is usually: 'Can I lift the spring bulbs before the leaves die down, to make room for summer bedding plants?' But of course that is no answer. The bulbs would have to be potted up or replanted in an out-of-sight corner to finish their growing season, otherwise flowering would be poor the following year; and in a very small garden where do you find a spare corner for 'heeling-in' bulbs, or room for pots of bulbs with untidy leaves? The only time to lift bulbs for storing dry is, naturally, once they have died down.

In any case, most bulbs resent annual lifting and drying-out and are better off, and quite happy, left in the soil all year round; except, of course, for tender bulbs which have to be lifted for the winter, and the large hybrid tulips which can contract tulip fire disease if left in the soil during summer. Moreover, if you start trying to lift bulbs and replace them with other things, you are climbing on the 'bedding out' treadmill, with all the trouble that this involves.

Obviously, since they do not need or like heavy summer waterings, these bulbs are generally best in the situations I have recommended. All but the most finicky ones, however, will be fine amongst perennials in the borders.

If they are packed in close to the perennials, then the summer plants will fill in the gaps as the spring bulb leaves start to die down in June. Where you have a large clump of something like daffodils, it is best to plant purposely around the bulbs with large and leafy herbaceous plants, to ensure good coverage of the bare patch. Do not cut or tie up the bulbs leaves (this can badly affect future flowering and growth); just allow the surrounding plants to cover them gradually, then clear the bulb leaves when they have yellowed. The roots of summer plants will, in a closely-packed planting, help to keep the soil around the resting bulbs dry. For this reason, I like to tuck spring and autumn bulbs right in amongst herbaceous perennials, sometimes actually amongst their roots; or even a bulb or two under the roots if I am planting bulbs and herbaceous plants at the same time in autumn.

I also like to have the spring bulbs dotted about in smallish clumps among the perennials, so that they pop up, flower, and then disappear quickly and easily in the froth of summer foliage and flowers. That does not mean that I dislike large drifts of bulbs, but these I prefer to keep towards the back of the border, where the leaves will be hidden later, or under trees and shrubs.

Bulbs which really do need to be in very dry soil during summer should be placed in the hottest and driest spots, close to warm walls and fences, in raised-up areas, under shrubs, etc. These include such fussy things as the tiny *Iris reticulata* varieties, *I. danfordiae*, *I. histrioides*, dwarf narcissus species like *N. bulbocodium*, tulip species (which can be left in the ground all year if they are in a dry position) and any bulb that you feel should not be risked in the hurly-burly of the general border planting. (See also Chapter Eight.)

Something else that I have tried recently with a fair degree of success is sowing hardy annual seeds around clumps of spring bulbs, to grow up and fill the gap as the bulb foliage dies down. Choose easy and strong-growing annuals, sowing them early in the spring, and watch that they are not smothered by the old bulb leaves as these flop over. Once again, the roots of the summer annuals help to keep the soil around the bulbs dry, but they must be tough hardy annuals which do not need pampering and will survive and bloom without very heavy waterings—plants like eschscholzias, nasturtiums, *Nemophila menziesii*, poppies, and viscarias. Sweet peas are also worth trying.

Summer-flowering bulbs are even better for interplanting and underplanting with herbaceous border plants. Tender ones like the large-flowered gladioli, tigridias and freesias can simply be popped in during late spring to add to the summer display. They do not have to take up much room, since they will spear up quite happily through low-growing perennials; when I use them as a summer boost, I simply pop the bulbs in as the herbaceous plants are starting to come up, right in amongst the other plants. The summer bulbs are frequently rather floppy-stemmed things which actually benefit from the support of surrounding plants—always provided that you work out the comparative heights beforehand: avoid putting the smaller bulbs amongst very tall,

leafy plants which will smother them.

Hardy summer bulbs, like the lilies, *Gladiolus byzantinus*, crocosmias, *Galtonia candicans*, the Dutch and English irises, are simpler still. They can go in as permanent plantings amongst shrubs and other plants, where they will enjoy summer watering as much as anything else in the border. These bulbs (particularly the lilies) prefer the soil to be on the dry side during winter and are safest in amongst the roots of other plants at that time of year, particularly if the soil is on the heavy side or the site very flat, low-lying and prone to winter waterlogging. Lilies, as I have said before, like their heads in sun but their roots shaded, and when they come up through other summer plants this fits the bill perfectly, in addition to providing support for their stems. These are ideal bulbs for 'cramming in' with other things.

There are places in my garden, and in other gardens that I know, where this interplanting and underplanting is taken to its limits in an attempt to squeeze as many plants as possible into a tiny area; where every square centimetre, even below the shrubs, is packed with plants; where, if you lifted the leaves of the larger plants, you would find tinier things spreading around; and if you had the courage to plunge a spade into the soil and lift out the closely-packed plants, you would find a layer of small spring bulbs within 4 or 8 cm (2 or 3 ins) of the surface, and below that another layer of deeper-planted lilies and other summer bulbs, colchicums for autumn, and goodness knows what else.

In fact, in my garden, I hardly dare use a spade at all for fear of what I might disturb, and I can barely do any planting these days without constantly referring to my bulb 'treasure maps', showing where each season's bulbs are hidden. Planting has become more of a delicate surgical operation, tentatively poking about with a trowel amongst the crowded plants and bulbs, hoping to strike gold in the shape of an empty bit of soil. And that is how I like it.

Even the grass is not spared in my craze for underplanting and making double use of what ground I have. Small spring bulbs sprout through the turf in one or two corners, producing a delightful meadow-flower effect in February and

March; turning the lawn into a lovely feature just when it would otherwise be looking its most bedraggled after months of rains and snow.

If you plant very early-flowering bulbs in a corner of the lawn, they will be dying down by late spring when the grass starts to need mowing. I like the hoop-petticoat flowered *Narcissus bulbocodium*, *Crocus chrysanthus* varieties (particularly the yellow 'E. A. Bowles' and 'Cream Beauty', which stand out well against the green of the grass), *C. tommasinianus*, and snowdrops. You will most likely have to do the first early grass mowing around them, since they will probably not die down completely until after the end of May or early June; but by the time summer really arrives, the bulb foliage should have yellowed enough to show that they can be mown down.

Should you have a small tree in the lawn, a few of these bulbs around its base will make an even lovelier feature for late winter and early spring. Here you could perhaps have a couple of tubers of the winter-flowering *Cyclamen coum*, its glowing ruby-red or deep pink flowers making a superb contrast with snowdrops in January and February. Grass around a tree can be left unmown for even longer without looking too untidy, and here you might also like some trumpet daffodils; I would heartily recommend the early-flowering *Narcissus cyclamineus* hybrid 'February Gold', at just 25 cm (10 ins) tall, and with a very neat little trumpet, a perfect small-garden plant. Where shrubs spread out over the lawn (as often happens in a small garden) it will not be too noticeable if a little patch of grass stays unmown until June, providing another possible home for some bulbs.

The autumn colchicums look good in grass under a tree, and they will thrive right up against the trunk, the mauve-pink goblet flowers spearing through the grass without any leaves in September and October. It is in the spring and early summer that the long, large leaves appear. These look handsome until they start to flop over and turn yellow in June or July, and they are less of a nuisance under a tree or large shrub than where the foliage may flop onto smaller plants.

Path planting
I know that I keep saying it, but a keen gardener working in a restricted area will be constantly looking for extra places to squeeze in a few additional plants, and an obvious choice is in gravel paths and drives, and in the crevices between paving slabs. It is amazing just how many things will survive and even romp away in such dry and trample-prone positions.

Obviously, you will not want to plant a path or patio so densely that walking along it becomes a game of hopscotch, but even just two or three small plants will greatly help to soften the look of gravel or paving, giving it a more mellow appearance. Where the cracks between existing paving slabs are so narrow that they make planting difficult, it is easier to slide in young seedlings, or even to sow a few seeds.

Garden steps may offer further possibilities. You might be able to squeeze a small plant or two into cracks between steps set into the soil, again to soften the harsh edges. Even concrete steps and doorsteps may boast tiny cracks where soil and weeds have collected over the years. Get the weeds out, pack in a little more soil, and plant a few seeds or seedlings here as well.

If grass and weeds will grow in cracks, then so will tough little plants, and on some shady concrete steps in my garden I have managed to establish primroses, *Corydalis lutea*, thyme, and the dwarf golden-flowered *Hypericum olympicum*, all growing in almost hairline cracks. Their roots plunge down into the soil below, and with regular watering and liquid fertiliser in the first year, they soon got a strong hold. The steps look that much lovelier for their fresh greenery and flowers.

I have even had some success in sowing a few hardy annual seeds into narrow cracks between steps and paving which were too small to plant in, but where I fancied a quick softening effect for the summer. I had the best results from the bright yellow and orange Californian poppies (*Eschscholzia californica* and *E. caespitosa*)—comparatively drought-resistant plants, as they would be, originating from a hot and arid climate. They needed plenty of water and liquid fertiliser at first, and the flowers were not as large as they would have been in the border, but there were plenty of them, carried over delightfully compact plants—less leaf and more flower, which cannot be a bad thing.

Elegant hardy annuals like the eschscholzias are my favourites; they are not too highly bred and 'improved', so that they retain much of the charm of the wild flowers from which they were raised and selected. They look good as summer border gap fillers, colourful enough to compete with any plant yet natural enough to look at home beside the classiest of flowers. They suit formal and informal plantings, look good in containers, and are particularly useful for filling empty patches of poor or stony ground (where they will seed themselves around). And you can simply sow them direct in the spring; no messing about with raising seedlings indoors or under glass.

I also like 'old-fashioned' sweet peas, the strains that still retain a heady perfume (more important to me than giant, frilly flowers). These I also use everywhere for summer colour; scrambling through and over perennials and small shrubs, climbing up anything and everything, and trailing over low retaining walls; I even plant a few seeds to grow up into one of my early-flowering clematis, to carry on the show when the clematis is over for the year.

Plants in containers
I prefer to see the rather fancier annuals and summer bedding plants—the petunias, salvias, pelargoniums, tender fuchsias and suchlike—restricted mainly to tubs, windowboxes and hanging baskets. Better this, I always feel, than to rely too heavily on them for extra colour in the border, where they only have to be replaced eventually.

Hanging baskets, tubs and other containers frothing over with these brightly coloured flowers can certainly add extra zest to a tiny garden in summer, particularly a paved town garden or courtyard where planting room in the ground is very severely restricted. Here, brackets could be fixed to walls and fences to hold small, lightweight plant troughs and pots, as well as hanging baskets, so that the colourful display is spread all around. Tubs and troughs may also be placed on garage and outbuilding roofs, filled with trailing plants to cascade down the walls in sheets of colour (in these situations, climbing annuals like sweet peas and morning glories will serve equally well as luxuriant trailing plants; and the same goes for windowboxes).

Container-planting is not just about annuals, bedding plants and seasonal bulb displays, however. Tubs, troughs and windowboxes can also provide homes for shrubs, climbers, and neat hardy perennials. So have a think before you allocate all the containers purely to temporary plants.

For permanent features in containers, evergreen plants are particularly useful. Tubs full of purely deciduous shrubs or herbaceous plants would be a dull waste of space in winter. Go for things like handsome-leaved evergreen shrubs (e.g. rhododendrons and camellias—but remember to use lime-free compost), or dwarf conifers with heathers and alpines. Tough evergreen rock plants, for trailing over the sides of tubs, include the dianthus (pinks), armerias, sedums and sempervivums, helianthemums, aubrietas, *Phlox subulata* varieties, *Alyssum saxatile* and the common thyme, *Thymus serpyllum*.

Tubs are also useful for planting climbers to cover walls where the ground is paved or concreted, but remember that the larger the plants, the more watering and feeding they will need. Shrubs, conifers and climbers may need daily watering in hot summer weather, especially if the container stands close to a wall or fence where it will be sheltered from rain. And since plant foods tend to wash quickly out of the fast-draining compost in containers, it is best to feed regularly with a balanced liquid fertiliser (six or seven times a year during spring and summer for shrubs and climbers; more frequently for fast-growing temporary plants like annuals). Liquid fertilisers with essential trace elements help to ensure healthy growth.

Garden soil should never be used in containers, as it may well contain insect pests and plant diseases, and it may be sticky and badly drained. Always use a good quality potting compost, preferably a reputable brand-named compost, rather than very cheap 'special offers' which may be of poorer quality (a few pence saved will not make up for disappointing plant growth). I have always

found that a standard peat-based compost will suit most temporary plantings, with extra grit or sharp sand added for plants that need particularly good drainage, like rock plants and bulbs. For more permanent plantings, such as shrubs and climbers, a loam-based compost like John Innes No. 3 is best, mixed with some extra peat. Drainage is also important: fill the base of a large tub with at least 5 cm (2 ins) of broken crocks, and cover them with peat or well-rotted manure to prevent the soil filtering through.

A good range of fruits and attractive vegetables may also be grown in containers, and good compost, regular watering and feeding are especially important here to ensure heavy cropping; but more about fruit and vegetables in Chapter Twelve.

Flowering hedges

Although I have touched briefly on hedges (and they will be discussed further in Chapter Eleven), I have not yet mentioned flowering and mixed hedges. These are two ideas which can help the owner of a small garden to achieve extra interest in a limited area.

If you are planting a new hedge, do consider using flowering or berrying plants—*Rosa rugosa*, berberis, pyracantha, cotoneaster, escallonia, etc. A hedge in a small garden should not just be a screen (although this is obviously important). Ideally, it should also provide interest and colour —either foliage tints (and many hedging plants change colour during the year) or flower and berry. The only trouble with flowering hedges is that you cannot trim them until after flowering and berrying are over; and in any case they flower and berry better if they are not kept poodle-neat all the time. This means that they will not be as tidy as a regularly-clipped foliage hedge, but with judicious pruning they can be kept within bounds and still make a lovely show. Some flowering hedges are not evergreen, which may be a deciding point; this is where my next idea comes in.

A home-made tub planted with alpines: Dianthus *'Whitehills' (sprouting from planting hole in side of tub),* Daphne cneorum *'Eximia' and* Armeria caespitosa *'Bevan's Variety'; the dwarf iris to the right is* Iris setosa.

Mixed hedges can be equally interesting. Consider a mixture, for a handsome year-round screen, of something like beech, an evergreen berberis, holly or laurel, intermixed with a deciduous shrub providing bright summer flowers, such as *Rosa rugosa*, *R. moyesii* or other tallish shrub roses, philadelphus (mock orange), flowering currant or even that old faithful, forsythia.

You might even fancy a complete mixture of all sorts—a sort of 'shrub garden hedge'. This is an interesting way to grow a few of those extra and larger shrubs that you have no room for in the garden. Here again, the effect would be less neat and tidy than a trimmed hedge, but the feature would be worth it. I have recently replanted one of my boundaries with a hedge of beech intermixed with tall, single-flowered shrub roses which I am hoping will send their arching shoots spearing out of the fresh green summer beech leaves in cascades of blush-pink blossom— something worth waiting for, and at no extra expense in terms of planting-space than a simple beech hedge alone would demand.

Foliage in the small garden

So far I have only given brief mention to foliage colours, forms, textures and contrasts. No doubt this is because, like most gardeners, the flowers provide the primary interest for me. Yet foliage plays a great part in the garden, particularly evergreen foliage, and I can admire and enjoy a good leaf colouring or shape as much as a bright and shapely bloom.

The plant world offers us an almost infinite variety of colours, shapes, and textures in leaf as well as in flower, and we can use these to make the garden more interesting. Apart from choosing plants with attractive foliage as well as flowers, we can try to arrange contrasting foliage schemes which will appeal to the eye even when the plants are not in bloom.

Leaf colourings of silver, grey, gold and cream will obviously be highlighted when planted alongside or, better still, in front of something of a darker tint, ideally a solid deep green. Pale leaf colourings (including silvers) also tend to be brightest in full sun. Shade often causes the foliage to produce more of the green pigment

41

chlorophyll which plants use to capture and harness the energy of sunlight for growth; the less sunlight, the more the need for chlorophyll, which makes pale-coloured foliage (including variegated leaves) darker and duller. This is a pity, since light foliage tints can be so useful for brightening up dark corners. If the shade is not too dense, variegated and light-tinted foliage plants are worth trying, but in constant dense shade they may be disappointing. In that case the best thing is to move them to a sunnier spot. If you want to experiment in this way with dark corners, pick the most silvery or the brightest yellow or variegated plants you can find; these will stand the greatest chance of retaining good colour in deep shade. Red and purple leaf tints also tend to be brightest in sun, and a little muddier when heavily shaded.

Leaf shapes, too, can provide fascinating contrasts, like a ferny or lacy, deeply-divided leaf alongside or in front of something with a bolder and rounder leaf form—a ferny-leaved *Dicentra spectabilis* against a large-leaved rhododendron, for example. Stiff sword-shaped leaves, like those of the irises, crocosmias, kniphofias and gladioli, can provide further contrasts with plants of a softer, bushier habit, and plants with tall and stately growth can be contrasted with lower, spreading plants. The permutations are infinite.

Look at the plants as complete entities, judging and evaluating their foliage as much as their flowers, and you'll soon come up with all kinds of combinations and contrasts of your own devising. And do not forget that even amongst green foliage plants there is plenty of variation and opportunity for attractive contrasts: pale greens and dark greens, glossy greens versus matt or felted greens.

Colour schemes

Of flower colour combinations and clashes I am going to say very little, since this seems to be very much a matter of taste; indeed, it is a matter of taste whether you worry about them at all. I seldom bother to plan colour schemes in great detail, although I suppose in a general way I try to avoid concentrating too many different strong colours together in one place (more for the sake of

having my strong colour splashes well spread around the garden than to avoid colour clashes). My approach is much more casual: I put plants where I think they will grow well (in sun or shade, under a shrub or in the open) and where I have the space. Ninety-nine per cent of the time nothing clashes violently with anything else (or if it does, I am so interested in the individual plants that I do not notice); and if a planting clash does look truly awful, then I shall perhaps do something about it later.

In any case, just about every gardener finds that some of his or her best plant combinations happen more or less by accident, without any great forethought. How much of that is due to pure coincidence and how much to unconscious inspiration is always debatable.

Room for fruit and vegetables

Where and how can you grow edible produce in a really small garden? Can you fit them in at all? At one time I did not think it possible in a very small space; I was more interested in flowering plants —until I rediscovered the immense pleasure (and health benefits) of eating fresh produce straight from the garden; for me, it was an almost-forgotten childhood pleasure.

When I acquired that first tiny garden of my own, my one thought was to make it as attractive as possible. Since I was so short of space, the thought of growing food barely entered my mind until the garden was already crammed to overflowing with flowers. And I did not want a vegetable patch spoiling the effect.

It did not take me long to realise what I was missing: fruit and vegetables far fresher and tastier than most of the stuff I could buy in the shops, and the most delicious varieties (not just what the commercial grower and the shop owner thought I ought to want); and all straight from the garden, packed with more vitamins than most shop produce could boast. Since those days, I have also discovered what many other gardeners

An excellent group of foliage contrasts : Acer japonicum *'Aureum' with dark conifers,* Salix *'Wehrhanii', the large velvety leaves of* Lavatera olbia *'Rosea' and the hand-shaped leaves of* Helleborus orientalis.

have long known; that growing your own fruit and vegetables in an organic way, with compost and organic fertilisers instead of chemical fertilisers, gives you a much tastier end-product.

But the main problem in a small garden is where to grow these things. Do you have a separate little 'kitchen garden' area for vegetables, fruits and herbs, or will this spoil the look of the garden? If you have only a few dozen square metres, or even less, outside the back door, a vegetable and fruit patch may be too prominent, and perhaps not terribly attractive to sit and look at on a summer's afternoon. Many people can derive great pleasure from seeing produce growing healthily, promising rich rewards for their labour (and I am one of them), but ideally a vegetable patch should not intrude on the rest of the garden. If there is room to screen off a small area with a hedge, then all well and good; but in very, very small gardens the only real answer is usually to try to grow a few of the prettiest vegetables and fruits 'cottage garden style', alongside and mixed with the flowers in the borders, and in tubs and other containers.

Fruit trees can be trained on walls and fences, alongside flowering climbers; so can blackberries, loganberries, redcurrants and hardy grape vines. Dwarf bush apple trees can be grown in the border or in tubs on a patio. Strawberries (particularly the delicious, small clump-forming and non-running alpine strawberries) make an attractive and tasty border edging, or they can be planted in tubs and deep windowboxes.

These are all good-looking fruiting plants which will not seem too out of place amongst the flowers; indeed, they will all contribute to the spring and summer display with flowers of their own, plus colourful fruits.

And there are plenty of handsome vegetables which will look equally appropriate in the flower borders, particularly if they are tucked away in sunny corners. Take outdoor tomatoes as an example: attractive ferny foliage and beautiful red fruits, and there are some superb dwarf bush varieties available now which need no staking and which produce tiny cherry-sized fruits that are a pleasure to see as well as to eat; if they were inedible berrying plants, gardeners would probably be falling over themselves in their haste to grow these 'large-berried' plants in the border! Tomatoes are of course also suitable for growbag or tub culture on patios, and the tiniest dwarf bushes may even be grown in windowboxes and pots.

Scarlet runner beans, with their hot red flowers, are one of the most delightful sights in the vegetable garden; there is certainly a place for them amongst the flowers, as colourful and productive climbers on sunny fences and walls.

Then there are the handsome dwarf French beans, not only green-podded but also intriguing purple and yellow podded varieties. In fact there are many pretty vegetables and fruits (not forgetting the culinary herbs, of course) that can be easily slotted into the ornamental garden without a separate kitchen garden patch. The possibilities will be discussed more fully in Chapter Twelve.

4
Choosing a Tree

There should be room for a small tree in even the tiniest of gardens, to add height and scale to the layout, but it is essential to select something that will not grow too big for the available space and which is unlikely to cast too much shade.

Siting the tree, or trees, should be tackled with equal caution. You might want something tall to hide an unattractive view, but take care that it does not block out all your sunlight at the same time; try to choose a tree that will grow high enough to act as a screen, but not so tall that it keeps the sun off the garden for half the day. If, on the other hand, you have a pleasant view from the garden, make sure that your tree is not positioned in such a way that it will eventually obliterate it. And the most important point is to ensure that the tree will not, as it grows, cast a lot of shade over your sunny sitting-out area. Always check on the speed of growth and ultimate height and spread, then try to imagine the tree in a few years' time. Is it likely to shut out most of your afternoon sun when it reaches maturity?

Planting your tree where it will cast some shade in the morning (or late evening) will not create anything like the problems of having your afternoon sunlight blocked out, so, generally speaking, look first to boundaries or areas of the garden to the north and east of your sitting area, or perhaps to the west, but only in desperation to the south. Do not, however, let worries about shade put you off planting a tree; remember that shade does move round during the day, and a small tree will only cast a pleasant dappled shade, in which your plants (and quite possibly you) will enjoy a brief respite from the blazing sun on scorching summer days. And on autumn, winter and spring

days, when we welcome every minute of sunshine, deciduous trees of course cast very little shade at all.

Flowering cherries

The flowering cherries have always been my favourites. Many of them are neat trees, ideal for the small garden and unfailing in their abundant spring display (and that's important; better that your one tree should be guaranteed to make a stunning show every year than that it should flower or berry one year and sulk the next). The blossom may be fleeting, but while it lasts it is superb. One of the most popular choices, for its deep purplish-pink colour and marvellously profuse flowering display, is *Prunus* 'Kanzan'. But this is one of the fastest-growing of the cherries, quickly exceeding 4.5 m (15 ft) and very likely to double that height eventually. It is also such a familiar sight in gardens that I am going to move straight on and look at one or two more adventurous choices.

Where space is limited, I would rather go for something a little slower-growing and more out-of-the-ordinary, like the elegant species *P. sargentii*, or the breath-takingly beautiful Great White Cherry, *P.* 'Tai-Haku'.

P. sargentii has to be one of the loveliest of all the cherries: it certainly gives the gardener immense value. The large, single pink blossom starts to unfold from late March to early April, enhanced by new leaves of a bronze-red tint; and, not satisfied with this display, *sargentii* proceeds to put on another colourful show at summer's end, taking on bright autumn tints of orange and red that rival the maples for fiery intensity. Add to that the undeniable fact that *sargentii* is one of the most graceful of the cherries, with trunk and branches of a glossy reddish-brown, and it ought to be high on any gardener's list.

If I were forced to choose between this and 'Tai-Haku', it would take me some time to make a decision. I should want to pick 'Tai-Haku', quite apart from its great beauty, so that I could tell visitors the romantic tale of how the 'Great White Cherry' died out in gardens and became a horticultural legend—until a single specimen (apparently the last one in the world) was discovered growing in a Sussex garden; from this all the 'Tai-Hakus' now bought and planted by gardeners originate. After that, to tell you that it is an extremely shapely tree producing a truly spectacular display of huge snow-white flowers fully two inches across, and that the young foliage is a wonderful contrasting coppery-red, seems rather prosaic and hardly does justice to such a ravishing beauty.

Although both of these cherries can, in time, attain the same sort of dimensions as 'Kanzan', they are slower-growing and comparatively neat trees, taking a fair number of years even to reach 4.5 m (15 ft). The same applies to the early-flowering 'Accolade', a lovely hybrid from *sargentii* with semi-double pink blossom in late March and early April. For something smaller, I would pick 'Shimidsu Sakura', a late-flowering cherry (April–May) with large semi-double white flowers tinged pink in bud, the petals attractively frilled around the edges. This is a very fine spreading tree, seldom more than 3–4.5 m (10 –15 ft) in height, widely branching and casting only light shade. 'Shirotae' is somewhat similar, bearing single or semi-double white flowers on slightly drooping branches; but it is rather larger all round, spreading sideways rather more.

If you fancy a weeping cherry, then the double pink 'Kiku-shidare-Sakura' (Cheal's weeping cherry) is probably the neatest choice at around 4.5 m (15 ft), with a similar spread. But this, like any weeping tree, does take up a fair bit of ground-space. The best answer is to put it in a corner and plant shade-loving things like primulas under it, or perhaps primroses, polyanthus and early spring bulbs like crocus, to give a display before blossom-time and the ensuing foliage hide the ground. On a general note, putting any weeping tree (particularly a willow) in the middle of a tiny lawn in a small garden is asking for trouble. Before you know it, you will be unable to walk round the blasted thing, and you will be forever cutting back the trailing branches so that you can mow under them. For the middle of a small lawn, stick to an upright tree, and tuck the 'weepers' away in corners.

Where you are extremely short of space, you might consider the thinly erect-growing 'Amano-gawa', a semi-double pale pink cherry which forms a narrowly upright column somewhat like a Lombardy poplar. This may eventually reach 6 m (20 ft), but only after about 20 years; and it never branches widely, restricting its spread to a metre or so, taking up little room and casting hardly any shade. Whether you regard this kind of columnar shape as a true substitute for a more natural spreading tree is a matter of taste. I always feel that it should be treated as a tall shrub rather than as the main tree for a small garden, especially where there is room for something more spreading. But there is no arguing with the fact that it is a real space-saver.

It is no wonder that cherries are the most popular trees for small gardens. Quite apart from their unrivalled spring display and their neatness, the cherries are so easy to please. They will thrive on virtually all types of soil, especially limy ones, provided they are not too wet. Even heavy clay or dry, stony ground will not put them off too much, especially if you give them a good start with plenty of peat or compost and a dose of compound fertiliser (and do not dig or hoe too much underneath them, because they are very shallow-rooting). Indeed, it is only sensible to take the utmost care over the planting of any tree; it is going to be one of the most important and permanent features of the garden, so it is worth taking trouble over it from the outset. Prepare the planting site well, feed and water regularly, and do not allow grass to grow up to the trunk until thoroughly established (at least three years).

Acer japonicum 'Aureum', a slow-growing yellow-leaved Japanese maple.

47

Slow-growing acers

After the cherries, my next choice would have to be from among the acers, unbeatable for autumn colours and wonderful leaf shapes. Some are regrettably too large for the small garden, but there are many suitable for even the tiniest of courtyards. Naturally, the smallest acers are also the slowest growers, but even as very young trees they are a beautiful and enthralling asset in any garden, always guaranteed to attract admiration.

Probably the best of all for a very small garden is the paperbark maple, *Acer griseum*; a slow-growing little beauty which, like *Prunus sargentii*, combines a number of attractive features in one tree, making it marvellous value for space and money. It is very nicely-formed, with evenly spaced branches and an 'open' head which does not cut out the sun too much; but the major features are its colourful peeling bark and its brilliant autumn leaf tints.

The bark continually peels away in large parchment-like strips, nutmeg-coloured outside and an amazing cinnamon-red within—a particularly enthralling spectacle on winter days or in the late evenings, when the low rays of the sun shine through the thin bark-strips, turning the tree into an illuminated outline of glowing red-brown tints. All summer the handsomely-cut leaves combine with the warm-coloured bark to create a real picture of a tree, always good to look at; then, as autumn draws in, the foliage takes on what must be some of the best autumn tints in the garden, a veritable bonfire-explosion of crimson and scarlet.

It takes the slow-growing paperbark maple many years to reach even 4.5 m (15 ft), so it certainly will not create any problems no matter how small the garden. Almost as slow and neat (up to 6 m (20 ft) in about 20 years) are the fascinating snakebark maples with their striking green and white striped bark. *Acer rufinerve* is the one I have, and this shows the white markings quite clearly on its bright green trunk even as a young tree. The autumn colours are also good, a mixture of reds and yellows. *A. davidii* is similar, best in the form sold as 'George Forrest', although the autumn-colouring leaves lack the usual lobed maple shape.

Smaller and slower still are the Japanese maples, *Acer palmatum* and *A. japonicum*. These are the best-known and most popular of all, and deservedly so, for they are wonderfully decorative things, offering the gardener a wide variety of summer foliage-colours and some of the most brilliant autumn tints in the entire plant kingdom. Some of the forms available are as tiny as any tree could be without having been subjected to bonsai treatment; many are shrub-size, and the largest forms will make tiny trees that will not outgrow even the most restricted spaces (seldom more than 4.5 m or 15 ft). All possess handsome, deeply-lobed foliage, almost feathery in the *A. palmatum* 'Dissectum' forms, where the leaves are finely divided almost to the base in a delicate ferny effect. The green-leaved forms are the best for autumn colour, bursting like fireworks into a blazing display of fiercely glowing reds, yellows and oranges. Forms with purple and red-bronze foliage are superb for summer colour, usually taking on brighter crimson tints later.

One of the most attractive (although they are all lovely) is the purple-leaved *A. palmatum* 'Atropurpureum', a strong grower which will, after a few years, make a small tree of about 2.5 m (7 ft) in height (sometimes more, given good soil and a sheltered spot). The spreading branches build up in a wonderfully architectural and classically beautiful way, fanning out into horizontal layers, one above the other around the slim trunk. As autumn approaches, the foliage gradually turns a richer crimson-purple hue, and even in winter the intricate pattern of the wand-like branches shifting in the wind is pleasant to see. For really bright autumn tints on equally neat little trees, the *A. palmatum* 'Heptalobum' forms 'Elegans' and 'Osakazuki' are superb, both turning brilliant sunset-tints of scarlet-red. These two also have particularly large and handsome leaves.

The *A. palmatum* 'Dissectum' forms, with their finely-divided leaves, are all much smaller, forming low, spreading mounds seldom much more than 1 m (3 ft) in height, even as aged specimens. These will be discussed later, as shrubs.

Of the *A. japonicum* forms, 'Vitifolium' (over 3 m (10 ft) eventually) is a superb choice for

Lilies are spectacular in a small area. Top left: Lilium 'Eros', one of the strongest growing and most beautiful of the new Scottish-raised lily hybrids; top right: Lilium martagon album, one of the few lilies that will tolerate fairly heavy shade; below: the Japanese Lilium auratum, L. speciosum and their large-flowered red, pink and white hybrids are superb for late summer and early autumn.

Spring beauty I. Above: The early-flowering Narcissus *'February Gold', an excellent small trumpet daffodil; below left:* Crocus tommasinianus *forms,* snowdrops *and* Eranthis *'Guinea Gold', marvellous dwarf bulbs for winter and early spring; below right:* Tulipa praestans *'Fusilier', a superb small multi-flowered tulip.*

Spring beauty II. Top left : Old-fashioned yellow polyanthus-primroses in March ; these are a sweetly scented strain raised from the old variety 'Barrowby Gem', flowering here with the lovely soft pink Primula sibthorpii; *top right :* Anemone fulgens *'Annulata Grandiflora' in April ; below :* Paeonia mlokosewitschii *in April.*

Spotlight outstandingly beautiful flowers by showing them off in isolation. Top left : Tulipa sprengeri, *a very late-flowering and wonderfully elegant species ; top right : the pasque flower,* Pulsatilla vulgaris, *flowering in the rock garden in April ; left :* Meconopsis grandis, *one of the blue Himalayan poppies, a thrilling sight in late spring and early summer.*

autumn colour, its large green vine-like leaves turning a bright crimson-red. 'Aureum' is a much slower-growing form (up to 2 m or 6 ft) with summer foliage of a soft sulphur-yellow colour, again turning red as autumn approaches.

All of these acers will tolerate some lime, although they do much better if liberal quantities of peat are dug into the planting site; this is particularly true of the Japanese maples. Ideally the soil should be well-drained but moisture-retentive in summer, so it is best to give them as much peat or compost as possible, whether the soil is limy or not. Annual feeding with a slow-release fertiliser like John Innes Base in early spring will encourage fast growth and good autumn tints; and the trees should never be allowed to get dry at the roots during their first few summers if you want to keep the growth going strong and obtain a good-sized specimen as soon as possible. But above all else, wind-shelter is the most important point to bear in mind. The larger acers will cope reasonably well with exposed, windy sites if the soil is well prepared as suggested; but the Japanese varieties may suffer badly in windy gardens if they are not at least partially protected; these should be tucked into the most sheltered corners available, where shrubs, trees, hedges or walls will help to screen them as they grow up; they will also appreciate a position where they will not receive full, scorching sun all day long, since they enjoy some shade during hot summer days.

The Japanese acers do tend to grow rather bushy in their early years, and as the tree develops you may find that a little careful pruning will improve the shape; not a 'short back and sides', of course, but a judicious thinning of congested branches to open the tree out a little and increase its graceful appearance, with perhaps the removal of any branches very low to the ground, to enhance the miniature tree effect.

Flowering crabs, mays and rowans

Flowering crab-apples have long been popular as small-garden trees, providing colour and interest in two seasons: late spring blossom, followed in the autumn by highly decorative, brightly-tinted red or yellow crab-apples which may be used to make tasty preserves. Some are very neat little trees which will not grow much more than 4.5 m (15 ft) with a compact head, and even the most vigorous should not exceed this in the first ten years.

Malus 'Profusion' (4.5 m–6 m or 15–20 ft) is the variety most often seen, its deep purple-red blossom making a striking show against the dark coppery-purple of the new leaves, with plenty of red fruits to follow in the autumn months. For something lighter and more airy in tone, you could not choose better than *M. hupehensis* (6–8 m or 20–25 ft), a real stunner in late May when its branches are laden with fragrant snow-white flowers, flushed with pink in bud. This is one of the larger varieties, but it is also one of the most free-flowering, and it produces a good crop of small cherry-like, yellow crab-apples tinged with red.

Where you want something really small, consider 'Red Sentinel' (3–4.5 m or 10–15 ft), a white-flowered variety with graceful arching branches and scarlet fruits which persist even after the autumn leaves have fallen, staying on the tree until late winter; long-lasting fruit is a valuable bonus in a small garden (always provided you do not pick it all for preserves). 'Red Jade' (3 m or 10 ft) is another with long-lasting red fruits that will hang on long after the leaves have gone; this is a neat little weeping tree with white blossom.

Of the pure yellow-fruited varieties, 'Yellow Siberian' (3–4.5 m or 10–15 ft) is excellent, and here again the fruits last well into winter. 'Golden Hornet' is a strong grower but stays smallish (4.5–5.5 m or 15–18 ft) with stiff, erect branches which do not spread too widely; and the crops of small crab-apples are both long-lasting on the tree and extremely heavy.

The crabs are not fussy about soil, although they prefer good drainage and benefit from soil improvement with peat or compost before planting.

Flowering mays or hawthorns are tough little trees thriving in poor soils and all kinds of situations and conditions. *Crataegus oxyacantha* 'Paul's Scarlet' (4.5–6 m or 15–20 ft) is the popular double-flowered deep rose-crimson, but there are also showy double pink and white forms.

The mountain ash or rowan is also neat (4.5–6 m or 15–20 ft) tough and easy to please. The white hawthorn-like spring blossom is not particularly showy, so the main features are of course the ferny foliage and the autumn fruits, usually sealing-wax red but sometimes yellow. *Sorbus aucuparia* 'Fastigiata' is an upright-growing, thin columnar form with red fruits; 'Asplenifolia' has very finely-divided and ferny leaves; and 'Xanthocarpa' (*Fructu-luteo*) is the yellow-fruited rowan whose berries seem to be less attractive to the birds than the typical red fruits, so that they frequently last into winter. But best of all is 'Joseph Rock', another yellow-berried form but with foliage that often turns a marvellous crimson-purple in autumn, providing a good backdrop to the butter-yellow fruits.

Robinia, birch and willow

Robinia pseudoacacia 'Frisia' (6 m or 20 ft) has become quite popular as a slow-growing small-garden tree, admired for its much-divided leaves, bright yellow in spring and turning just a little greener as summer progresses. This does well on dry soils, including chalk, but the colouring is very unusual and you should really see it 'in the flesh', rather than relying on catalogue or book descriptions, before deciding whether or not you can live with it.

Silver birches are attractive trees, slim in outline, and casting only light shade; but their roots are greedy, spreading far and wide just under the surface of the soil, so that the more vigorous of the birches can rob a fair area of the garden of valuable summer moisture. They also tend to become infested with aphids in hot seasons, and these little pests excrete copious amounts of sticky honey-dew which can become a real nuisance, particularly if it drips all over your parked car or a picnic lunch. These are, of course, points which could cause problems in the very smallest gardens. However, there is no denying that *Betula pendula* 'Tristis' (7.5–9 m or 25–30 ft) is a beautiful tree with its silver trunk and slender drooping branches, while *B. pendula* 'Youngii' is a smaller, though less elegant, weeper (train to desired height on a stake).

The willows also have greedy and spreading roots, only the very tiniest being even remotely suitable for the smallest gardens, for instance *Salix caprea* 'Kilmarnock' (or 'Pendula') a rather stiff little thing with congested branches (3 m or 10 ft). *S. purpurea* 'Pendula' (3 m or 10 ft) is a more graceful small tree with purple-grey shoots, thriving in dry situations.

An excellent alternative would be the weeping willow-leaved pear, *Pyrus salicifolia* 'Pendula', a compact little tree (2.5–3 m or 8–10 ft) which gives the effect of an extremely silvery-white-leaved weeping willow; with creamy-white flowers and small brown fruits when mature.

Evergreen trees

Small broadleaved evergreen trees are unfortunately far and few between; there are plenty of conifers, of course, but so many of the tree-sized ones are simply too large for a very small garden, while the neatest are more like shrubs.

Of the few broadleaved evergreens that are available, probably the most desirable for a small garden is the strawberry tree, *Arbutus unedo*, a slow-growing little treasure with glossy dark-green leaves, bright red shoots and rough reddish-brown bark; as handsome in leaf as the frost-tender bay tree. This starts life more as a shrub, but in time will make a small tree never more than 4.5 m (18 ft) tall except on the richest soils in the mildest counties. Lovely as the leaves are, symmetrically spaced spiral-fashion along the colourful shoots, it is naturally the small orange-red strawberry-like fruits for which this tree is best known. The white or pink flowers appear in late autumn, and the fruits generally do not develop until twelve months later during the following autumn, so that many a gardener has waited excitedly for fruits when his or her tree first flowered, only to be puzzled by their non-appearance. But the disappointment is usually made up for the following year when the fruits do finally appear, often at the same time as the next batch of flowers, in October or November.

A sheltered position is best for the strawberry tree, perhaps close to a sunny house wall or in a cosy corner protected from the cold north-easterly winds of winter. It is hardy enough once established and growing strongly (particularly in sheltered town gardens), but very young specimens may suffer some frost damage in severe winters if placed in an open and exposed situation. If cold-weather damage does occur in an exposed garden, protect the young tree with netting or sacking during severe freezes. Prepare the soil thoroughly with plenty of peat or compost and John Innes Base to encourage speedy development; the strawberry tree will tolerate limy conditions, but will grow faster and taller with some peat in the soil.

The hollies (*Ilex* species and forms) have always been a popular choice for neat evergreen trees as well as shrubs, but they generally need to be planted in pairs, a female bush with a male form, to ensure pollination of the flowers and resultant berrying on the female holly. However the forms 'J. C. van Tol' (3 m or 10 ft), 'Pyramidalis' and 'Pyramidalis Fructu-luteo' (both 4.5 m or 15 ft) are all females which berry heavily on their own; and they are also smooth-leaved and prickle-free. The first makes an upright, slightly columnar tree with red berries, the second two (as the names suggest) form narrow upright conical trees, the berries on 'Pyramidalis' being red, and on 'Pyramidalis Fructu-luteo' a bright yellow. These can be treated as shrubs when young, the lower trunks being 'cleaned up' later when they approach tree height.

As I mentioned in the previous chapter, there are a few large shrubs which eventually grow into small trees with a good spreading head, particularly when the lower branches are trimmed off to give a cleaner trunk. Of these, some of the taller cotoneasters provide useful evergreen or semi-evergreen foliage as well as valuable winter berries.

Cotoneaster 'Cornubia' is a typical example, reaching 4.5 m (15 ft) in as many years, with wide-spreading branches. The large leaves are semi-evergreen, lasting right through the winter if the weather is not too harsh or if the garden is sheltered; even in a bad winter, they can usually be relied upon to clothe the branches well into January and February. The bunches of waxy red berries ripen in autumn and are equally persistent, providing winter decoration right through

almost to spring. A large specimen in a garden near me held both foliage and berries throughout the terrible arctic freeze-up of 1984–85, only starting to lose a few leaves and berries in February; and it was still fairly well clothed with old leaves as the new shoots sprouted in the spring. *C. frigidus* (3.5 m or 12 ft) is similar, but less reliably evergreen; however, it still holds its old leaves well into winter along with its red berries. 'Exburiensis' and 'Rothschildianus' (both around 3 m or 10 ft) are reliably evergreen, a little slower-growing, with yellow berries.

More tall shrubs which make good substitutes for trees in the tiniest gardens will be discussed in the following chapter, but to end with here, let us take a quick look at the larger conifers.

All fast-growing conifers are, by their very nature, forest trees, ultimately rocketing up to great heights and also broadening out considerably at the base; the smaller the garden, the more you should be wary of them. And in the tiniest gardens only the true slow-growing miniatures are really safe to plant; anything that grows fast enough to make a small tree within a few years will soon get out of hand where space is limited. There are so many, all with varying rates of growth and ultimate heights, that it would be impossible to go through them all here, so the best I can do in a general way is to stress the importance of checking good reference books like *The Hillier Colour Dictionary of Trees and Shrubs* before buying.

However, if you are thinking of planting a fast-growing conifer as a tree (as opposed to low-growing bushy ones), then in a small garden it is better to look at the tall, thin spire-shaped or columnar types rather than the more bushy or widely-branching ones. There are quite a few of these, all of great architectural beauty and useful for adding height to the garden layout, whilst taking up little ground-space and casting a minimal amount of shade. I know that I said the columnar broadleaved trees did not seem quite like true trees to me (e.g. *Prunus* 'Amanogawa'), and that these were perhaps better considered as tall shrubs. With conifers, however, a tall, thin spire-shape is far more natural and acceptable to the eye; although where there is little room for trees, I still like to see a shapely spreading tree as the main feature, with such things as columnar conifers playing a secondary role.

A typical example would be *Chamaecyparis lawsoniana* 'Columnaris', a small tree reaching perhaps about 3 m (10 ft) in as many years and very slim and elegant with a spread of only around 60 cm (2 ft) at the base; the young foliage is silvery-green, deepening to a greyish-blue-green. The junipers also boast some attractive spire-shaped trees, like *Juniperus communis* 'Hibernica', the Irish juniper; this will eventually reach about 3 m (10 ft) or more with very neat, dense foliage like a clipped yew; and the juniper 'Skyrocket' (2.5 m or 8 ft) is slimmer still, seldom more than 30 cm (1 ft) wide at the base. Speaking of yews, there is also the densely columnar Irish yew, *Taxus baccata* 'Fastigiata', a handsome little tree (3–3.5 m or 10–12 ft) with even darker green foliage than the larger and more sprawling common yew.

Where there is room for something bushier, as a screen at the end of the garden, or tucked into a corner at the back of a wide border, the following are all unlikely to grow more than 3 m (10 ft) in about ten years, but will spread more at the base and therefore take up more growing space: *Chamaecyparis lawsoniana* 'Ellwoodii' (never much more than 3 m or 10 ft), grey-green in summer, blue-grey in winter; *C. lawsoniana* 'Fletcheri' (4.5 m or 15 ft eventually), feathery grey-green foliage; *C. lawsoniana* 'Stewartii' (6 m or 20 ft after many years), pyramidal shape and golden-tipped foliage; *Cryptomeria japonica* 'Elegans' (4.5 m or 15 ft eventually), a delightful bushy little tree with soft, feathery foliage, fresh green in summer, turning purple and bronze-red in winter.

5
Shrubs for Small Gardens

There are a great many tidy little shrubs which should be of particular interest to owners of small gardens, some of them truly dwarf and safe to plant even alongside the daintiest rock plants. The smallest shrubs are of course marvellous when it comes to squeezing that proverbial quart into a pint pot that has become an obsession with me, so allowing the keen gardener to cram in more plants for a greater variety of form, foliage and colour, as well as for interest in different seasons. But no matter how small the garden, it would be a rather flat and boring place if it contained only the tiniest and tidiest shrubs available, with nothing a little larger and more exuberant to provide that equally important variety of scale and height.

Although the small-scale gardener should obviously concentrate as much as possible on neat shrubs, there should also be room for a little extravagance; for one or two really stunning larger shrubs. This is not a matter of robbing the available planting space if you consider that, no matter how large the shrub, it can always be underplanted, as discussed in Chapter Three; in effect you do not really lose much more than the small area immediately around the trunk or base.

Where space is a problem, the spread of a shrub is as important as height, if not more so. Always check before buying and planting. But do not be afraid to put them fairly close together, so that eventually they start to spread into one another a little.

Like all plants, shrubs are gregarious things, quite happy growing shoulder-to-shoulder and even through one another. In particular, young shrubs benefit from fairly close planting, helping to shelter one another from the sharp frosts and drying winds that can sometimes cripple a newly-planted shrub in a more isolated and exposed situation. Follow the basic rule of not planting large and fast-growing sprawling shrubs next to slow-growing small things, and you should not have any real problems. You may not always end up with perfectly-shaped specimens as some of the shrubs grow into one another, but I think that is more than made up for by the luxuriant effect of almost solid thicket-like growth—always more natural and pleasing to my eye than a regimented array of perfectly-spaced and perfectly symmetrical 'specimen' shrubs growing in carefully-arranged isolation.

There should always be a place for one or two individually-sited 'feature' shrubs, stunning and precious things that you might want to see standing out from the hurly-burly of the main plantings; but every shrub cannot be an isolated feature if you want to squeeze in as much as possible and achieve that luxuriously overflowing effect.

Allow room for the shrubs to put on a reasonable amount of growth before they start to join hands (first checking up on estimated spread) so that they do not make a thicket and strangle one another while they are still young and struggling to become established. But do not leave such a wide margin for development that they will take forever to fill it. In a small garden, you will no doubt find that there is no room for this in any case. And if things do get too congested and overgrown after a few years, you can always move (or even remove) one or two shrubs; better that, I always feel, than to stare at a garden full of blank gaps for years on end, while you wait for widely-spaced shrubs to mature. Even if you have to discard two or three of the fastest-growing shrubs in the end, to ease the overcrowding, surely the pleasure you will have had over the years will be worth the few pounds that they cost. It certainly will not have been money wasted.

Like the trees, shrubs will be comparatively permanent features. As such, they deserve more care and attention when planting (and in subsequent years) than you might perhaps give to herbaceous plants which can be more easily and safely moved, replanted or divided if they are unhappy or in the wrong place. With large subjects like trees and shrubs, avoiding problems is always better than trying to cure them later. Quite apart from considering height and spread when selecting planting sites, make sure that you choose plants to suit the situation and the soil —shade or sun, dry soil or damp conditions, limy soil or acid. And make the soil improvements prior to planting as thorough as possible.

All shrubs will benefit from some peat or compost in the soil to help them get started, although many are deep-rooting and, once established, will tolerate dry soils very well; exceptions will be mentioned as I come to them. Unfortunately, few small shrubs will put up with very badly-drained ground, and in this situation, lots of peat or compost should be used to lighten the soil; with perhaps some sharp sand or grit as well, to further improve the drainage where the problem is particularly bad.

Certain shrubs, like the rhododendrons and camellias, will not of course grow in limy soils. Where there is lime in the ground, these lovely things can be planted either in tubs filled with lime-free potting compost, or in raised beds made up of peat, sand and fertiliser (or even in large pockets of this lime-free mixture, in the ordinary garden border).

Although the usual advice to gardeners living outside our mildest coastal counties is to stick to reliably hardy shrubs, it is worth remembering that small, closely-planted gardens (and especially those protected by surrounding walls and buildings) are often more sheltered than larger and more open gardens in the same area. So, if you feel that the garden is reasonably sheltered, it

can be worthwhile and exciting to experiment with one or two more tender things in warm corners; and this applies particularly to enclosed gardens in the heart of a town or city, where winter temperatures tend to be a little higher than in rural areas.

Tall shrubs as tree substitutes

First of all, as promised in the last chapter, we shall look at some more tall shrubs which will grow into elegant small trees, suitable for gardens where there is no room for many (or any) full-sized trees. These are superb for adding height to the layout and producing a tree-filled effect without ever becoming tall. All can be treated as attractive shrubs at first, eventually removing lower branches, if necessary, to produce a cleaner trunk as they grow taller. Most are also very open, lightly-branching things which will not cast dense shade.

One of my favourites is the Mount Etna broom, *Genista aetnensis*. This will quickly shoot up to around 2.5 m (8 ft) if well fed and watered, eventually making a small tree up to 4.5 m (15 ft) in height. It is easily trained as a standard, producing a very open head of thin, drooping branches which carry summer leaves so tiny and sparse that the sun shines through almost unhindered, allowing plants and other shrubs to grow happily around its feet; and in July it is a fragrant fountain of golden broom-flowers that scent the air far and wide. The bonus is that it thrives on poor, dry soils, and its arching whipcord-thin branches look good all year round as they bend and sway with the slightest breeze.

Stranvaesia davidiana is another beauty, a semi-evergreen of a similar open and lightly-branching habit, throwing dappled shade as it grows. This will also reach about 4.5 m (15 ft) after many years, the stoutly upright stems allowing for underplanting if cleared of lower branches.

The stranvaesia's spring foliage is always colourfully tinted bronze-red, followed by white

Genista aetnensis, *the Mount Etna broom, flowering in late July; eventually it makes a small tree like this, with tiny leaves that cast virtually no shade.*

hawthorn-like blossom in June and red berries ripening in August and September, at which time some of the old leaves also start to turn the brightest scarlet-red imaginable, falling gradually as winter advances, to form a glowing carpet on the ground below. Yet enough leaves (both green and red) remain on the tree throughout winter to keep it from looking bare.

What more could you ask from a shrub—or a tree? I suppose you would also like it to be easy and fast-growing, suitable for poor, dry soils, limy or non-limy; tolerant of city pollution, perhaps; or equally happy in a sunny position or in shade? That is asking a lot! But, as it happens, it is all of these as well.

Amelanchier laevis and *A. lamarckii*, the June berries or snowy mespilus, are stunning deciduous shrubs which also make small trees in time. Both produce masses of snowy-white flowers in spring, with sweet berries to follow in July (black in the case of *lamarckii*, and crimson berries on *laevis*). The brilliant orange-scarlet autumn leaf tints are superb on both shrubs, and the young spring foliage on *laevis* is also a lovely coppery-pink. These two succeed best on non-limy soil, not too dry; but they will tolerate slightly limy ground (not dry chalk) if planted with plenty of peat around the roots. The only problem with them is that the birds love the sweet berries, so these do not last long.

The deservedly popular *Magnolia soulangeana* will, given time, make a wonderful large shrub or small tree, although some pruning may be necessary to encourage it to add height rather than spreading sideways too much where space is a problem; start with a tall specimen, near to standard-tree size if possible (you will find tall plants if you shop around), train it from the start, and you will soon have a very neat and lovely little tree that will be no problem anywhere. And what a sight the huge white and rose-pink tulip flowers are, one of the glories of spring. This is, of course, quite happy on limy soils (although it will always appreciate some peat when planting) but not on shallow chalky ground.

Finally, two gorgeous tall viburnums. *V. bodnantense* is a valuable winter-flowering shrub, carrying its strongly fragrant clusters of pink-flushed flowers on bare branches from late autumn right through to spring, so good for cutting and bringing into the house. This is a fairly tall, narrow-growing shrub, spreading out at the top into a good semblance of a tiny tree, especially when trimmed a little around the base. *V. bodnantense* 'Dawn' is the strong-growing form usually offered. *V. burkwoodii* is one of the best evergreen garden shrubs you can plant; its pink-budded white flowers are gloriously sweet-scented and produced in clusters against the glossy green foliage during April and May. Both do well on limy soils.

Evergreen shrubs

With their year-round foliage, the evergreen shrubs form the backbone of any garden, so there should always be a fair number of these, preferably well distributed around the garden to contrast with the deciduous things and to act as permanent screens and windbreaks.

Lime-hating flowering shrubs for spring

Spring is a season dominated by some of our loveliest evergreens. I refer of course to the rhododendrons; and before those who garden on limy soils throw up their arms in despair, I am going to repeat what I said at the beginning of this chapter: lime-haters like the rhododendrons, azaleas, camellias and pieris can be grown quite successfully in tubs or raised beds filled with a peaty, lime-free mixture, should the garden soil be too limy for them.

The lime-free 'ericaceous' potting compost sold by garden shops and garden centres is excellent; or a home-made mixture of peat (moss peat is the best) with plenty of sharp sand or grit (lime-free of course; check on this when buying) plus some John Innes Base fertiliser, will do equally well. To ensure good drainage, you really need about one bucketful of sharp or coarse sand (or fine grit) to every three buckets of damp moss peat, well mixed; and do not forget the fertiliser. Adding composted bark will further improve the drainage and texture, but is not essential.

Rhododendron moupinense *flowering with the snowdrops in late winter.*

A raised peat bed for lime-hating shrubs need not be very deep, since these shrubs are quite shallow-rooting, their roots tending to stay in the peat layer rather than growing down into the limy soil below; as little as 15 cm (6 ins) will do except on the very limiest soils (i.e. chalk) where a depth of at least 30 cm (1 ft) would be safer.

Nor does the peat bed have to be particularly large, perhaps only big enough for a couple of superb lime-hating shrubs and plants. Where the soil is only slightly limy, these shrubs may even be planted in ordinary borders, in pockets of lime-free mixture large enough to take the roots with plenty of room to spread.

In any case, these lime-haters do not actually need very acid soils; they will thrive quite happily if the ground is only slightly on the acid side, or even neutral; so it is worthwhile checking your soil with an inexpensive pH testing kit (test different parts of the garden, because the soil can vary even in small areas).

Perhaps the shrubs will not grow quite as strongly under these conditions as they would in a natural, deep non-limy garden soil, but they can still be superb. In my limy garden I have rhododendrons and camellias growing quite happily in patches of peaty soil in the borders, and they make a stunning show every year without fail.

Rhododendron moupinense is one of the first to flower, in February and March, an elegant small-leaved shrub never much more than one metre (3 ft) in height. The flowers are delicate, fragrant, wide-open funnels, white flushed with pink and lightly freckled in the throat with carmine-red. It is best in a sheltered spot amongst other shrubs or close to a high wall, where the precocious blooms are less likely to be spoiled by sharp frosts. Another of my favourites is 'Cilpinense', a hybrid from *R. moupinense*. The flowers are similar but appear later, usually in April, and are therefore less prone to frost damage, making this a good early-flowering choice for a cold or exposed garden. As for height, it is a little smaller even than *R. moupinense*. A popular choice for early colour is the dwarf *R*. 'Praecox', bearing masses of bright purple-pink flowers in late winter, so also best in a sheltered spot amongst other shrubs. These are all free-flowering.

There are one or two dwarf lavender-blue or violet-blue rhododendrons, generally blooming in April or May; keep an eye out for *R. scintillans*, 'Blue Diamond' and 'Bluebird'. And of the dwarf yellows, you cannot beat 'Yellow Hammer', a truly dainty and low-growing shrub with clusters of delightful lemon-yellow bell-shaped flowers in late April and May; or there is the creamy-yellow flowered 'Cowslip', a nice little dome-shaped bush. Of the red-flowered dwarf varieties, I would recommend the free-flowering 'Elizabeth' and 'Scarlet Wonder'.

R. williamsianum can sometimes be a rather shy-flowerer, but it is an attractive dwarf species with bronzy-coloured young leaves and bell-shaped pink flowers in April. Luckily there is an equally neat pink-flowered hybrid from it, 'Bow Bells', which is good in May.

But if there is to be just one dwarf rhododendron in the garden, it should without doubt be *R. yakushimanum*. This marvellous Japanese species slowly makes a tight dome of darkest green leaves, 60 cm (2 ft) high, a superb backdrop to the clusters of large appleblossom-pink flowers which appear in late May or early June—more like the huge flower trusses of one of the tall hybrids than the flowers of a tiny shrub. These are followed by the new leaves, covered in a beautiful silver-white woolly coating and providing yet another enchanting contrast with the older and darker foliage. A really first-class shrub.

If one or two of the earliest-flowering rhododendrons are best in a sheltered spot, the same applies even more strongly to the dwarf evergreen Japanese azaleas; although reasonably hardy, they are liable to be cut by severe frosts in exposed situations, and the April flowers are particularly sensitive to late cold snaps. A position sheltered from north-easterly winds and amongst taller shrubs, or below the protecting branches of a tree, is essential, as is shelter from early morning sun which will rapidly thaw frozen leaves and flowers and increase the damage. The range includes some pretty garish hues as well as some softer colours, so always choose your plants in flower.

The other great group of spring-flowering,

lime-hating evergreens is of course the exotic camellias, once considered too tender for outdoor culture but now firmly established as reasonably hardy garden shrubs.

The *C. japonica* and *C. williamsii* varieties are the toughest, perfectly happy when given a sheltered spot, and particularly if grown as wall shrubs. It is the early spring flowers which may be harmed by sharp frosts, so, like the evergreen azaleas and the earliest rhododendrons, the camellias are best where they will not be caught by early morning sun; that rules out walls facing east. Camellias also prefer shade, so a west- or north-facing wall is ideal, although any situation which gets a little shade during the hottest part of the day will do. If planting against a shady wall, remember that shelter is needed from cold north-easterly winds, and a very exposed and windy north wall will not be suitable. Naturally, planting amongst other shrubs will help to provide shelter.

Planting camellias in tubs, to stand against a wall on a path or patio, is a good idea, but camellias (and rhododendrons) need plenty of moisture during summer, and they are more prone to drying out at the roots in a tub than in the open ground; in a severe winter the roots of camellias in tubs are also more likely to be damaged by frosts than they would be in the ground. Keep them well watered during spring and summer and move them to a shady spot if possible; and in severe winters protect the roots by covering and wrapping the tubs with sacking or other insulating materials.

The *C. williamsii* varieties are the hardiest, vigorous but compact, and 'Donation' is one of the loveliest with its large semi-double silvery-pink blooms; my plant came through the dreadful arctic winter of 1984–85 completely unscathed and flowered unprotected, tucked in close to a hedge which provides shade for most of the afternoon. This is a very neat, upright-growing shrub which never demands a lot of space, and the glossy leaves are good to see at any time of year. There are many other varieties, doubles and semi-doubles, pink and white, but none lovelier than this.

Almost as hardy, the *C. japonica* varieties come in a far wider range of doubles, semi-doubles and singles, whites, pinks and reds. 'Adolphe Audusson' is a stunning deep rose-red semi-double, strong-growing but compact. And another beauty is the single white 'Alba Simplex', also a neat shrub.

Flowering times vary from one variety to another, and from season to season, but you can expect to see buds bursting any time from late winter to late spring. Very early flowers are best picked for the house if sharp frost is forecast.

The pieris are much sought-after for their brilliant red spring shoots, but these refined-looking evergreens are attractive to see all year round. *P.* 'Flame of the Forest' (or 'Forest Flame') is one of the neatest and hardiest, as well as one of the most colourful. The young leaves start scarlet-red, slowly turning more pink, then cream, and finally green as summer progresses. The white spring flowers are carried in arching sprays a little like lily-of-the-valley. A shady and sheltered spot in lime-free soil or peat is essential, and in such a situation 'Flame of the Forest' will slowly, over a period of about ten years, make a 1 m (3 ft) mound. It may double that with good, deep soil and plenty of shelter from winds and frosts, but only after a great many years.

Lime-tolerant evergreens for spring

Many gardeners no doubt associate fragrance in the garden mainly with summer days and evenings, yet spring has some delicious scents to offer, and in a small garden we should take advantage of these whenever possible. Top of the list come the daphnes, and in particular the dwarf evergreen *D. retusa*, a magnificent little shrub that takes up almost no room at all yet scents the air for metres around in May. This is by nature an alpine shrub, equally at home in the rock garden or at the front of a bed, where it very slowly swells into a tightly-packed mound of dark evergreen leaves, never much more than 60 cm (2 ft) high. The small fragrant flowers are white flushed with rosy-purple, freely-produced, waxy and long-lasting. *D. tangutica* is similar, not quite such a dense bush and with slightly longer and more pointed leaves, of a marginally lighter shade of green; interesting to grow alongside *retusa*.

Even tinier—and definitely a plant that demands pride of place in the rock garden, at the edge of a raised bed or some such 'special' spot —is the highly fragrant mat-forming garland flower, *D. cneorum*. But since this really is more of a rock plant, I shall just mention it here and discuss it more fully in Chapter Seven.

Osmanthus delavayi is yet another wonderful spring-fragrance shrub, one that will swamp the entire garden with a sweet daphne-like scent on warm, still April days. The flowers, too, are daphne-like; tubular and starry-mouthed, pure white against the dense glossy-green foliage. The leaves are small and closely packed, almost as neat as a trimmed box hedge. Although larger than the evergreen daphnes, this is a very slow-growing shrub, likely to reach no more than 1.5 m (5 ft) in its first ten years.

Similar, but a little faster-growing, is *Osmarea burkwoodii*, a hybrid between two different shrub genera, osmanthus and phillyrea; which explains its great similarity to *Osmanthus delavayi*, since this was one of the parents. It flowers at the same time with the same fragrant white flowers and much the same dense green foliage. But the osmarea benefits from hybrid vigour, often reaching 2 m (6 ft) in the time that it takes the osmanthus to attain 1 m (3 ft). Yet it is still a very neat and tidy shrub which will not gobble up a great deal of space. The other parent, *Phillyrea decora*, is also worth looking out for, as slow-growing as the osmanthus, white flowered and fragrant.

Skimmia japonica is a popular tough, slow-growing shrub with scented white flowers in March and April; good for a shady corner, but a male and a female plant are necessary if you are to get the bright red berries in autumn and winter.

Finally, one for a sheltered border, preferably against a sunny wall: the Mexican orange, *Choisya ternata*. This may be cut by frosts during severe winters, particularly in cold or exposed gardens, so (although it will recover from frost damage) a wall bed is the safest bet. Given a warm corner, it should reach about 1.5 m (5 ft), the sweetly-scented white orange-blossom flowers appearing in late May and during early summer. The foliage is a very glossy dark green.

All of these spring-fragrance shrubs are, thankfully, happy on limy soils; and the same goes for the spring-flowering dwarf evergreen berberis. Most of the barberries are largish shrubs, and many are deciduous. But there are one or two neat little evergreens, like *Berberis stenophylla* 'Corallina', a mass of red buds and yellow flowers which last for weeks on end during late April and May, on a 1 m (3 ft) bush of small dark leaves. *B. stenophylla* 'Coccinea' is very similar, but its red buds open a glowing orange-pink. Smaller still is the variety 'Corallina Compacta', a truly dwarf shrub for the rock garden, with apricot-yellow flowers. All thrive on poor, dry soils, in sun or shade.

Summer-flowering evergreens
Of the early summer-flowering evergreens, my favourites are the sun roses; the cistus species and varieties. For a non-stop display throughout June and July, they really are hard to beat, perfect for filling the gap between the last of the spring flowers and the main summer season. All are small, spreading shrubs and, although they have a reputation for being not completely hardy, mine came through the harsh winter of 1984–85 very well. Out of nearly a dozen plants, only a couple were cut back by frosts, and those quickly made new growth. The poorer and drier the soil, the tougher they are and the better they flower, so use them to fill your hottest, most parched corners; those patches of stony ground where you would not expect anything to thrive.

It is fascinating, the way these shrubs burst their buds so fast, the delicate single rose flowers unfurling in the morning so quickly that by noon they are wide open to the sun, while the petals are still endearingly crinkled from their recent confinement—like crumpled tissue paper slowly unfolding before your eyes. (Indeed, if you watch carefully and long enough, you can sometimes actually see the petals uncurling, as you can with the fast-opening evening primroses.)

The one drawback is that each bloom lasts only for a day, the petals suddenly falling like confetti

The silvery-white young shoots of Rhododendron yakushimanum, *one of the best rhododendrons for a small garden.*

in the cool of the evening; but to make up for this, they come in a constant stream of unfurling buds, never a day without a host of new flowers, week after week.

Most of the species are white flowered, often with yellow centres or crimson blotches at the bases of the petals, and all are worth growing. However, the most popular are the pink hybrids 'Anne Palmer', 'Silver Pink', 'Peggy Sammons', *pulverulentus*, *purpureus* and *skanbergii*. Of these, 'Silver Pink' is probably the best all-round garden plant, one of the hardiest, limiting itself to a height and spread of about 60–90 cm (2–3 ft), and with glistening silky-pink flowers up to 7 cm (3 ins) across.

The hebes are also popular for summer colour, although here again you may find that they are cut back by severe winters; do not worry, however, because most sprout quickly from the base and recover, particularly if, like the sun roses, they are planted in the driest and hottest spots in the garden.

Hebe 'Autumn Glory' is a good dwarf evergreen for late colour, producing its intense violet flower spikes from July right through to autumn; the stems and leaves are tinged with purple. This and the even neater *H*. 'Carl Teschner', with its violet-blue spikes freely produced in June and July, are both reasonably hardy. Another hardy one that I find particularly elegant and lovely is 'Bowles' Hybrid', a very tidy little shrub no more than 45 cm (18 ins) tall, with delicate lilac-blue sprays throughout summer. But then all the hebes are as neat as any gardener could wish, and all are worth trying in a warm and well-drained situation. Feeding with sulphate of potash seems to increase their frost-resistance somewhat, and the same goes for the sun roses and any other not-quite-hardy shrubs and plants; at least it appears to work well in my cold, exposed garden.

Lavenders are useful summer-flowering evergreens for border-edgings and dwarf hedges, and they go well with the above shrubs, enjoying the same dry soils and hot situations; besides, it is always nice to have one or two aromatic-leaved shrubs in the garden. 'Hidcote' is one of the neatest and most free-flowering varieties, an attractive silvery-grey bush with dark violet

spikes. The escallonias, too, revel in dry soils, contributing a profusion of rose-red or pink flowers from late spring to autumn, 'Apple Blossom' being one of the most compact and free-flowering; these are also good for low, flowering hedges.

All the summer-flowering shrubs mentioned so far are happy on limy soils, but the *Calluna vulgaris* varieties, the most widely planted summer heathers, demand lime-free conditions. However, if the garden soil is neutral or acid (or if you are prepared to give them plenty of peat in a limy garden) these are excellent low-growing evergreen ground-cover plants. A well-drained and sunny site is essential, and they will not tolerate dense shade. Although, once established, they do well on dry ground, they do need a little pampering with peat around their roots to get them started. The golden-leaved varieties are particularly useful for foliage contrast and for year-round colour.

By selecting a range of early and late flowering varieties, it is quite possible to have colour from the callunas right through the summer and into October and November. Those that carry on the display until autumn are especially valuable, including the late flowering deep pink 'Peter Sparkes' and 'H. E. Beale'.

Evergreens for autumn and winter
For colour from autumn into winter, the berrying shrubs are invaluable, and the cotoneasters have always been a popular choice. I have mentioned the tall, tree-like varieties, but what about the low-growing spreaders, so useful for ground-cover on poor soils and for covering low walls and fences? The most widely planted of all, *Cotoneaster horizontalis*, is deciduous, but there are one or two evergreens that are especially good for year-round foliage cover as well as bright berries. *C. congestus* is one of the neatest, making a slow-growing ground-hugging mat suitable even for a rock garden, although it is most useful as a trailer down a retaining wall, or trained up a low wall. Small pink flowers are produced in spring, followed by clusters of red fruits. More vigorous creeping evergreens suitable for taller walls or ground cover include *dammeri*, *microphyllus* and

'Coral Beauty'; these are all wide-spreading red-berried cotoneasters that will climb to a fair height when trained on a wall or fence. All are good in shade.

Brighter still in berry are the pyracanthas or firethorns, equally good on walls, either in sun or shade. But these are bushier shrubs than the cotoneasters, requiring more careful siting. The pyracanthas are tall shrubs, often reaching 3 m (10 ft) in ten years and bushing out considerably at the base when grown as free-standing specimens. The varieties 'Orange Glow' and 'Orange Charmer' are fairly upright, but where space is a problem, even these are best against a wall, where the vigorous growth can be trained upwards and the base kept neat.

Regular trimming all over will reduce berrying, but with a wall for support the top growth can be left more to its own devices, to flower and berry freely, while the lower growth is restricted to keep the valuable ground-space below free for other plants. When pruning is necessary, this is best done immediately after flowering in June. But it is still wiser to avoid planting pyracanthas on walls beside busy paths where, even with trimming, their bushy habit could prove a problem; better to choose a less frequented wall area or a corner between two walls which the pyracantha can fill with white summer flowers and autumn berries in a less restricted fashion.

Despite being a little space-hungry, the pyracanthas are still about the best shrubs for berrying, the brilliant fruits persisting right through autumn and winter, often lasting until March; well worth squeezing into a small garden even if you do have to think carefully about a planting site.

Another rather space-grabbing shrub which should be squeezed up close to a wall or into a corner is *Fatsia japonica*, the ultimate in evergreen foliage plants with its foot-wide hand-like leaves. It may need thinning out and cutting back from time to time, but this is not much trouble. White globe-shaped flower heads are produced in October or November; it is best on a shady wall.

Anything which, like the pyracanthas, provides colour in winter should be seized upon, including that old favourite *Mahonia japonica*

with its handsome spiky leaves and lily-of-the-valley-scented yellow flower sprays. Its hybrid offspring *M.* 'Charity' is better still, a deeper yellow in flower. Both bloom from January to March and are good-looking foliage shrubs for the rest of the year; but they can become quite large and are best tucked into a corner at the back of a bed, where they will not become a nuisance; they can also be pruned back hard in spring if they do get out of hand. *M. aquifolium*, the Oregon grape, is a little neater, flowering later in March and April, with blue-black berries to follow. All do well in the deepest shade.

The sarcococcas (Christmas box) are useful low-growing and shade-loving evergreen shrubs producing small but fragrant white winter flowers. *S. humilis* is a dense little suckering bush with attractive shiny leaves and red-brown stems, not much over a foot in height.

Best of all for masses of cold-season colour in a small space are the neat winter-flowering heathers, the lime-tolerant *Erica carnea*, *E. darleyensis* and *E. mediterranea* varieties. In actual fact, the flowering season continues well into spring, since these tidy little heathers bloom over such a long period.

The first to start flowering, in late November or December, are the *Erica darleyensis* varieties 'Arthur Johnson' and 'Darley Dale', both rich rose-pink; these two are also the longest-flowering, often staying in colour right through the winter until April or even early May. Both are just over 30 cm (1 ft) in height and quite vigorous spreaders.

The *E. carnea* varieties are slower growing and usually less than half the height of the *darleyensis* types. Flowering commences in late December or January with the rosy-pink 'Winter Beauty'; 'Springwood Pink' is a little later, a very prostrate-growing variety. One of my favourites is 'Vivellii', also slow-growing, with very dark bronze-green foliage and deep crimson flowers, in colour from March to April. But there are many more to choose from, including the golden-leaved and pink-flowered *aurea* and the charming 'Springwood White'; grow as many as possible for non-stop colour throughout winter.

Finally, the *E. mediterranea* forms. The best to

my eye is 'Brightness', a good pale pink in flower over a long period from March to May; it makes a little shrub about 45 cm (18 ins) tall and as much across on my shallow limy soil, but up to 90 cm (3 ft) on deeper soils.

Although these heathers will all tolerate lime, they do not do so well on shallow chalky soils unless planted with lashings of peat; in fact, whatever the soil type, a little peat around the roots at planting time is advisable, to get them off to a good start; particularly on very heavy soils or very dry ground. Like the summer heathers, they must also have an open and sunny situation, not a shady corner.

The most reliable berrying hollies were discussed in the last chapter, as small trees, but naturally these will make neat shrubs in their early years, handy for winter colour; as they grow larger, however, they can take up a lot of room, so are probably best trained as standards eventually. And do not forget the tall, evergreen tree-like cotoneasters and their autumn–winter berries, which I also mentioned in the last chapter; and the semi-evergreen stranvaesia and the fragrant evergreen *Viburnum burkwoodii*, discussed at the start of this chapter; all are superb shrubs which, although large, may be squeezed into corners at the back of the border, with their lower branches cleared for underplanting, like small trees.

Deciduous shrubs
Spring-flowering shrubs
Having started the evergreen season with the rhododendrons, what else could we kick off with here but the deciduous azaleas? Strictly speaking, the azaleas are now classified by the botanists as part of the genus rhododendron, and nowadays you will often find them listed under rhododendron in many books and catalogues. However, from the gardener's point of view, the differences are important enough to ensure that the name azalea will continue in common usage for a very long time to come.

Unlike the dwarf evergreen Japanese hybrids, the taller deciduous azaleas are completely hardy, although of course they must have the same lime-free soil (or peat bed treatment in limy gardens) as the evergreen azaleas and rho-

dodendrons; like those shrubs, too, they prefer a shady position in the garden and plenty of summer moisture, so do not stint on the peat when planting. Shelter from drying winds when young is also important, so tuck them in amongst other shrubs.

Unfortunately, many of the modern hybrids lack the delicious scent of the wild golden-yellow *Azalea pontica* (now *Rhododendron luteum*) which I regard as one of the loveliest of all the spring shrubs; so if there is room for only the one azalea, you could do a lot worse than plant this 'ordinary' fragrant yellow. It is also one of the easiest to grow, succeeding better than most of the hybrids where conditions are not ideal, and the foliage takes on good scarlet autumn tints. A very elegant, fairly upright shrub, it is suitable for underplanting and not resentful of a little hard pruning when necessary.

The Ghent hybrids, like the neat-growing yellow 'Nancy Waterer' and the orange-red 'Coccinea Speciosa', are derived from the wild yellow and most have inherited both its sweet scent and its rich autumn leaf colouring. They are smaller in flower than many of the 'improved' hybrids seen nowadays, but the fragrance more than makes up for this as far as I am concerned; and they are as elegant in growth as their wild parent. The same comments apply to the fragrant and pastel-coloured Occidentale hybrids, like the delicate pinks 'Irene Koster' and 'Exquisitum'.

Magnolia soulangeana I mentioned earlier as eventually making a small tree, and it is certainly one of the most stunning deciduous spring shrubs with its huge tulip-flowers; but it does spread quite a lot and therefore, where space is tight, it is best pruned and trained from an early age to keep it fairly upright (even with a definite trunk). The ordinary white and pink type is the most reliable for poor, dry soils and limy gardens. The other superb magnolia for a small garden, *M. stellata*, is so early-flowering that I shall leave it until we come to winter.

One of the neatest and most free-flowering brooms for spring colour is *Cytisus praecox* 'Allgold', a solid mass of bright yellow flowers the whole length of the neatly arching shoots in late April and May. The ordinary, creamy-coloured

Hard to beat, if you only have room for one tree:
Prunus 'Tai Haku', the 'great white cherry'.

Summer profusion I. Above: Part of the author's small garden in early August. Lavatera olbia *'Rosea' provides splashes of bright pink all summer and into the autumn. Left: A tiny town garden in June. The polyantha rose 'Yesterday' on the left, with* Rosa alba *'Königin von Dänemark' on the right and 'The Wife of Bath' behind. Candytuft provides colour in the centre.*

Summer profusion II. Right : A small walled garden on two levels, packed with roses, clematis and small shrubs and perennials. Fuchsias grow in pots on the retaining wall. Below : Part of the author's garden, with lilies, Hypericum olympicum *and penstemons providing much of the colour.*

Two excellent shrubs for the small garden. Above: Camellia williamsii *'Donation', one of the hardiest of the camellias; a young specimen flowering freely in early spring. Left: The hardy fuchsias provide long-lasting colour for late summer and autumn; this is one of the best,* 'Mrs Popple'.

type is equally free with its flowers, and a nice soft contrast, but a little stronger growing. *C. kewensis* is even more compact, suitable for trailing over the edge of a rock garden or raised bed; it is semi-prostrate in habit, seldom more than 30 cm (1 ft) high, producing a wealth of creamy-primrose blooms in May. *C. beanii* is equally tiny and suited to the same situations; golden-yellow in flower.

Spiraea arguta is as easy to please on poor soils as the brooms, and just as free-flowering. Commonly known as May foam or bridal wreath, it is a slender shrub with arching, almost weeping branches that, in late April or May, burst into a solid foaming cascade of snowy-white hawthorn-like blossom from topmost branch to the ground; a marvellous sight.

For some really strong early colour in the spring garden, the japonicas or Japanese quinces have always been a popular choice. These tough and thoroughly hardy varieties of *Chaenomeles speciosa* and *C. superba* are best trained on a wall or fence, since otherwise they make sprawling bushes. All bloom from late March or early April to May, with pink or red flowers, the most striking being the deep reds like 'Rowallane' and 'Cardinalis'. Best in sun, but will tolerate a shady wall. The fruits can be made into preserves and jams.

And for something really exotic in late spring, you could not choose better than a tree paeony; the only trouble is that the brightly-coloured pink, red and white shrubby *Paeonia suffruticosa* varieties need a very sheltered spot shaded from early morning sun if they are to avoid frost damage to the young growths. Luckily the yellow-flowered *P. lutea ludlowii* is hardier and easier to grow, with highly ornamental deeply-divided pale green leaves that contrast well with darker and more solid shrubs; it blooms in late May or June.

As we move closer to summer, there is a fragrant daphne that should not be forgotten: *D. burkwoodii*, a larger shrub than the evergreens but still a very neat little bush usually not more than about 90 cm (3 ft) high and across. I almost included this with the others, as it is supposed to be semi-evergreen; but I have always found that it

can become so bare in winter (especially in a harsh one) that it is better counted pessimistically as deciduous.

As a young shrub, *burkwoodii* tends to be rather leggy and bare towards the base, but the heavenly scent from the pale pink tubular flowers in late May and early June is too good to miss. Nipping out the soft young shoots in spring will encourage it to grow bushier, and very leggy specimens are best planted deeper than they were in the pot; like *D. cneorum*, *burkwoodii* enjoys this treatment, rooting from the buried lower parts of the branches, and sometimes sprouting new shoots from the base. Plant in a sunny position for best flowering, and keep well watered during its first year because it may struggle in dry conditions.

I have mentioned some dwarf evergreen barberries for spring flowers, and I think this is the place to bring in the low-growing deciduous *Berberis thunbergii* 'Atropurpurea', so useful for purple-red foliage colour during spring and throughout summer. This is good as a small shrub or a low hedge, the colour becoming even richer as autumn approaches. Various other varieties are available, all neat shrubs with wine-red or purple-red foliage, including the truly dwarf 'Atropurpurea Nana' at just 30–45 cm (12–18 ins). The dwarf willows are also good foliage shrubs for spring and summer, with the bonus of attractive catkins. The woolly willow, *Salix lanata*, is probably the best-known, of a low, spreading habit with yellow-grey catkins in early spring and downy silver-grey leaves which look good against darker foliage. *S. hastata* 'Wehrhahnii' is taller, up to 1.25 m (4 ft), with green leaves and large catkins in April, which start silver-grey and quickly turn yellow with pollen; a very architectural shrub with handsome red-brown stems which are good to see even in winter.

Deciduous summer shrubs

When choosing the summer shrubs what we are really looking for is a long flowering season. In spring, autumn and winter, even a short burst of colour is welcome provided it is exciting enough; but summer-flowering shrubs face so much competition from border plants, and perhaps from annuals and suchlike, that the gardener may feel a little cheated by something shrubby that takes up valuable growing space in return for only a fleeting display.

Top of the long-flowering league come the shrubby potentillas, providing us with a succession of single rose-flowers from late spring to early autumn. Some may grow to 90 cm or 1.25 m (3 or 4 ft) and spread widely, but any that get out of hand may be cut hard back in March. *Potentilla fruticosa mandschurica* is very neat, almost prostrate, with grey foliage and non-stop white flowers. *P. arbuscula* 'Elizabeth' is taller but still compact, one of the best long-flowering yellows. 'Red Ace' is the much-applauded and comparatively new flame-red variety; this last one tends to fade to a lighter colour in very hot weather and droughts; keep it well watered at such times, and give it plenty of peat around its roots when planting.

The abelias are also good for a long display, the best being *Abelia grandiflora* and *A*. 'Edward Goucher'. These are supposed to be semi-evergreen but tend to lose the majority of their leaves except in the most sheltered and warm gardens. They are best against a warm wall, where they will get some frost protection and grow larger and more floriferous. Both produce lilac-pink flowers continuously from July to September and are graceful little thin-branched shrubs.

Of the hypericums, 'Hidcote' is superb, a constant source of gleaming golden saucers from July to October and easy on any soil; but beware *H. calycinum*, excellent low ground-cover for dry shade but a rampant spreader and likely to get out of hand in a small garden, spreading by underground shoots. Another good yellow for summer-long colour is the late-flowering broom *Cytisus nigricans*, just 90 cm (3 ft) tall with erect branches and not too bushy, ablaze with golden flowers from July to September.

A lovely accompaniment to these bright yellows is the pink mallow-flowered *Lavatera olbia* 'Rosea'. This is a very fast-growing shrub, superb for quickly filling a gap in the garden, capable of putting on 1.5 m (4 ft) of growth in one summer if regularly watered. Yet it can be chopped back

down almost to ground-level in early spring to keep it neat, and the never-ending stream of large pink flowers from midsummer to late autumn is an absolute delight.

It may be tempting to hack the floppy branches down in autumn as the flowering display ends, but the lavatera is not completely hardy and it is better to leave drastic pruning until April. If the shrub looks particularly untidy in autumn, I limit myself to lopping the top quarter off the longest and floppiest shoots, to make them less top-heavy and less liable to be flattened by heavy winter rains and wind. Having said that the shrub is not completely hardy, my own plants came through the bad 1984–85 winter all right in my cold and exposed garden; much of the top-growth was killed but, after a spring haircut and some prolonged rain, they soon recovered.

In a small garden I feel that roses should be long-flowering, highly fragrant, neat and shapely shrubs suitable for the mixed border, and preferably with additional features like colourful autumn hips.

One rose that fits the bill perfectly is *Rosa rugosa*. This is one of the most heavily scented roses you can plant, flowering freely in June and July and continuing to provide colour and fragrance intermittently right through to autumn, at which time the large globular hips turn orange-red. The variety 'Rubra' is a pleasing single crimson-purple, but even lovelier are the double 'Roseraie de l'Hay', the single pink 'Fru Dagmar Hastrup', the single white 'Alba' and the semi-double white 'Blanc Double de Coubert'. These are some of the neatest shrub roses, never growing very large and of an upright and sturdy growth that is ideal for mixing with other shrubs and plants.

Rosa moyesii 'Geranium' is also good, with its tall sturdy branches and its bright pelargonium-scarlet flowers in June and July, followed by some of the best rose hips of all: 5 cm (2 ins) long flask-shaped fruits that turn as bright a red as the flowers. This is a much more compact variety than the typical *R. moyesii*, the latter being rather large for a small garden.

The long-flowering scented hybrid musk roses are also neat little shrubs, and one of the best is

'Ballerina', about 1.25 m (4 ft) high and as much across, making a neat hummock of foliage smothered with single apple blossom-pink blooms non-stop from July through to autumn.

The *Gallicas* or French roses are some of the most colourful of the old-fashioned hybrids, making low, suckering bushes with few thorns, suitable for poor soils. Richly scented, they bloom in June and July and may be used for low hedges. My favourites are the double, deep pink 'Cardinal de Richelieu' and the single pink 'Complicata'. The China rose hybrids are also excellent, perpetual flowering from early summer to the frosts, forming compact, upright bushes with double or single blooms followed by scarlet autumn hips; 'Mutabilis' is a beauty, with single flowers that start out flame-red in bud, changing colour as they open, to apricot and pink. Hillier's (see Useful Addresses at the end of the book) is a reliable source for these old roses, as well as for the single-flowered shrub roses mentioned above.

Miniature roses have enjoyed a surge of popularity recently, probably not unconnected with their immense suitability for small gardens. Most put on their main display in June and July, with repeat performances from time to time during later summer. The one I have grown and enjoyed for years is the double shell-pink 'Cinderella'; this never grows more than 30 cm (1 ft) high, making a neat, rounded bush, and it blooms for me endlessly throughout summer.

Rosa rubrifolia is another little gem; the small single pink flowers are rather fleeting in June, but this is made up for by the attractive silvery-purple colouring of the summer foliage, the freely-produced red hips and the elegantly arching red-purple, almost thornless shoots. To demonstrate just how generous this rose is with its hips, the first time I saw it, a youngish plant spotted from a distance, the small red hips glowing along the full length of every arching leafless autumn branch, I thought at first that it was some kind of superlative deciduous cotoneaster.

Having mentioned summer fragrance with regard to *Rosa rugosa*, I cannot very well omit the sweet-scented mock orange or philadelphus. 'Beauclerk' and 'Belle Etoile' are two of the best larger varieties, both large-flowered singles and

highly fragrant. Where space is very tight, the mock orange fragrance can be enjoyed via one or two smaller varieties: the tiny 'Sybille', just 90 cm–1.25 m (3–4 ft) tall, with single purple-centred white flowers; *microphyllus*, 60–90 cm (2–3 ft), single; the pineapple-scented 'Erectus'; or the double-flowered dwarf 'Manteau d'Hermine'. For continuous free-flowering, remember to prune out shoots which have bloomed once the display is over, to make room for new flowering shoots to develop for the following year.

Deciduous shrubs for autumn and winter

For late summer and early autumn the hardy fuchsias are excellent, long-flowering and safe from the hardest winter frosts if planted deeply; in cold gardens, young pot-grown plants should have the lower leaves carefully stripped off, and then they should be almost buried, with the bottom half to three-quarters of the stems under the soil, to ensure that they are deep enough to come through bad winters.

All the hardy fuchsias are deciduous except in the mildest counties, and the old stems should be cut down in spring to make room for new growth. Heavy spring watering and liquid feeding will speed up development and encourage an early start to flowering. They are suitable for poor, dry soils and for the sunniest corners on heavy clay, provided you give them plenty of peat when planting and, as suggested, heavy watering in spring and early summer to get them going. Flowering usually starts in late June and often continues until the autumn frosts; in mild seasons as late as November.

'Mrs Popple' is the best all-round garden plant, one of the hardiest, growing to about 60 cm (2 ft), with large red and purple flowers on nicely arching stems over a very long season; if there is room for only one, it should be this. 'Tom Thumb' is equally hardy and reliable, but a true miniature, producing slightly smaller red and violet flowers on tiny bushes less than 30 cm (1 ft) in height. There are others worth trying in well-drained, sunny beds, like the semi-double 'Margaret' and the red and white 'Alice Hoffman', but none are as long-lived and reliable as 'Mrs Popple' and 'Tom Thumb'.

The hardy deciduous ceanothus are also useful for late colour, the best being 'Gloire de Versailles', a largish shrub best planted hard up against a sunny fence or wall, or tucked into a back-of-the-border corner, where it will not flop about so much; it may also be pruned hard in April, removing all the previous season's growth to within a few centimetres of the old wood. The powder-blue flowers appear from June to October.

The caryopteris and ceratostigmas are neater blue-flowered deciduous shrubs for late summer and early autumn. They do best in sunny planting sites, preferably close to the protection of a wall or fence in very cold gardens. Keep them tidy and free-flowering by cutting the previous year's growth hard back in April.

Caryopteris clandonensis (also commonly known as blue spiraea) makes a small bush about 90 cm (3 ft) high and wide, producing clusters of light blue tubular flowers during August and September. 'Heavenly Blue' is an even more compact variety, with darker flowers.

Ceratostigma willmottianum (the hardy plumbago) grows to roughly the same dimensions, with handsome diamond-shaped leaves and a succession of rich gentian-blue flowers from July through to the autumn frosts. *C. plumbaginoides* is a very dwarf species, growing to 30 cm (1 ft) with a spread of about 40 cm (15 ins).

Another late-flowerer best squeezed up against a sunny wall or fence is the shrubby mallow-flowered *Hibiscus syriacus*; this has a fairly compact, upright growth habit and the large blooms provide exotic colour from midsummer to October. Named varieties available include 'Woodbridge', a reliable rose-pink, and 'Blue Bird', a good large-flowered lilac-blue.

Leaf tints, berries and fruits are an important feature of shrubs in autumn. These have already been covered to a large extent in this chapter and the previous one, but there are a few shrubs that I ought to mention before we move on to take a look at one or two deciduous flowering shrubs for winter.

Most importantly, there are the Japanese maples that I mentioned briefly in the last chapter; the *Acer palmatum* and *A. japonicum* varieties,

unrivalled for handsome summer foliage and autumn tints. All those mentioned in Chapter Four stay shrub-size for a fair number of years, but the neatest for a very small garden are the diminutive *Acer palmatum* 'Dissectum' varieties which remain delightful little bushes with finely-cut leaves. The soft, feathery green foliage of 'Dissectum' itself makes a cool contrast to heavier-leaved evergreens like rhododendrons, turning orange-red in autumn. 'Dissectum Atropurpureum' is usually even more in demand for its dark, ferny bronze-purple foliage. Both look better in raised beds than in ground-level borders, especially when placed at the top of a low retaining wall where they can tumble downwards.

I have already discussed evergreen cotoneasters, but the deciduous *Cotoneaster horizontalis* is well worth a mention here since its autumn leaves turn a good crimson-red before falling, in addition to its plentiful red berry crops. It can be trained to as much as 2.5 m (8 ft) up a wall or fence and, although it does not provide winter greenery, is a fast grower which will cover unsightly objects quickly, the leafless but dense branches making a reasonable camouflage screen even in winter.

Of the autumn-colouring and berrying barberries, a neat-growing choice is *Berberis wilsoniae*; this makes a bush about 90 cm (3 ft) high and across, with russet-red autumn tints and masses of coral-red berries following the yellow summer flowers. Most of the others are rather large for the small garden and suitable only as flowering and berrying hedges.

Another shrub with good autumn foliage is the Chinese witch hazel, *Hamamelis mollis*, its broad leaves often turning a bright yellow. This is also one of the best winter-flowering shrubs, the sweetly fragrant golden-yellow flowers appearing on bare branches from January to March, and sometimes even in December. Better still is the much sought-after sulphur-yellow variety 'Pallida', free flowering and of a more delicate hue. Both will eventually make largish shrubs but are slow-growing to start with and stay fairly neat for

Magnolia stellata *flowering in March with a hedge of* Cryptomeria japonica *'Elegans' as a backdrop.*

a number of years; and even when they do become larger (up to 2 m (6 ft) or more), they tend to form graceful little trees suitable for underplanting.

The deciduous *Daphne mezereum* is a very neat and colourful shrub for winter, forming an upright little bush of about 90 cm (3 ft) in height, hardly spreading at all; it flowers in February and March on bare branches, with attractive but poisonous red berries to follow. Flower colour varies considerably, from washy lilac-pink to purplish-red, so it is best to buy plants in bloom, keeping an eye out for a good strong colour.

This shrub is also prone to a disease which stunts and twists the leaves and flowers, often producing a pale mottling of the young foliage. These are typical symptoms of a virus disease, which seems a likely cause since greenfly are about the only serious pests that attack this daphne, and they are carriers of plant viruses.

I have seen many plants offered for sale in this condition, and I hope no one buys them. Any newly-bought plant which shows these symptoms should be got rid of immediately (preferably back whence it came, with a strong recommendation that it be burned to prevent further spread of the disease) and a healthy specimen should be sought from a different source, since if one daphne in a nursery has the disease, it is likely they will all have it. Do not be fooled by the disappearance of the symptoms during summer; that can happen with plant viruses, but they will reappear the next spring and, in the meantime, may infect any other daphnes in the garden. Having said all that, a healthy specimen of this shrub is a joy in late winter, so do not be put off it.

Lovelier still is the white form, *D. mezereum alba*, flowering at the same time and producing bright yellow berries (again, poisonous). I grow the form 'E. A. Bowles', or Bowles' white mezereon as it is also known, a very free-flowering and particularly graceful plant which lasts for weeks in bloom and produces a very heavy crop of golden-yellow berries. The sweet fragrance is wonderful on a winter's day and therefore, whether you have the white or the pink, the best place for it is near the front door where you can enjoy the scent every time you pass in or out (and,

generously, share it with the postman).

When describing magnolias earlier, I mentioned the winter-flowering *Magnolia stellata*. This is a shrub that I should be glad to see in every garden, particularly the smaller ones, for it gives so much for such little growing room.

Stellata is a dainty little shrub, or rather a miniature and slow-growing tree; in ten years it might reach 90 cm or 1.25 m (3 or 4 ft), and you could wait more than half a lifetime for it to attain its maximum height of 3 m (10 ft). But fortunately this little beauty makes a stunning show even as a tiny youngster. In February the furry buds start to swell, and in March they suddenly begin to burst open, covering the plant in a galaxy of large, starry white blooms. And even when the show is over, *stellata* remains a handsome and airy-looking shrub throughout spring and summer, its pale green leaves providing a fresh and spring-like contrast against shrubs and plants of a darker foliage hue.

Finally, our look at deciduous shrubs for winter would not be complete without a quick reference back to the fragrant winter-flowering *Viburnum bodnantense*, suggested on p. 56 as a largish shrub suitable for treatment as a small tree. Although tall, it is reasonably upright and tidy; and, like all those tree-forming shrubs, it will make a neat enough shrub for a few years before you have to start thinking about perhaps clearing a few low branches to allow for underplanting.

Variegated shrubs

This is one of those subjects that revolves very much around personal likes and dislikes. Some people love variegated shrubs and cannot get enough, while others loathe them or like them only in moderation. In a small garden, I certainly feel it is best not to go overboard on shrubs which depend purely on variegated foliage for their one-and-only, never-changing attraction.

If you do have a craving for variegated shrubs or plants, they should ideally have other attributes to offer, or should serve a dual purpose in the garden—for instance a variegated ivy can provide a little colour and can also hide an ugly wall, or a variegated holly like 'Golden King' will have winter berries and perhaps also make an evergreen screen to hide an ugly feature or view. Incidentally, the popular *Ilex* 'Golden King' is, despite its name, a berrying female holly; it requires a nearby male for pollination and heavy berrying, such as that other misleadingly named holly 'Golden Queen' (male).

Many variegated shrubs (and plants) are, in my view, rather duller and less exciting 'in the flesh' than the vivid descriptions sometimes painted of them in books and catalogues might lead you to believe, and some can be downright disappointing. As with everything else, in a small garden you should hunt out the best from amongst the mediocre because there simply is not room to spare for disappointments. For example, 'Golden King' is the brightest where hollies are concerned (also not too spiky); and of the popular variegated *Elaeagnus pungens* varieties, 'Maculata' is by far the most colourful; these are also both comparatively slow-growing.

Dwarf conifers
Most of these comments apply equally to the smaller shrub-size conifers. Many are useful for evergreen foliage colour, for screening purposes and sometimes (in the case of the most shapely ones) as architectural plants; but, as with the variegated shrubs and plants, there is a bewildering range of varieties available, some good and some decidedly not so good. It is easy to make too much use of conifers in a small garden; like many of the variegated shrubs, they do not actually *do* much—except grow bigger and bigger (and that is a problem in itself if you do not choose slow-growing varieties). The more you have of them, the less room there will be for more interesting plants, those that alter with the seasons and make the garden an ever-changing and exciting picture.

The following are some of the neatest and best shrub-size and dwarf conifers (including ground-covering prostrate varieties) suitable for a small garden. The taller kinds look particularly good with heathers and other low-growing shrubs and plants like cistus, potentillas, helianthemums and hebes. The tiniest and slowest-growing types are safe to plant with alpines in a small rock garden or raised bed. All prefer a well-drained soil with plenty of peat around their roots when

planting. Raised beds and banks suit them well, and here their handsome shapes can be best appreciated. In hot summers, dwarf conifers may become infested with red spider mites or conifer spinning mites, tiny pests which cause foliage to yellow and then die back or fall; sprinkling the foliage when watering in hot, dry weather will discourage these pests, and in severe cases spray with malathion.

For golden foliage colour and a good conical shape, few conifers can rival *Thuja occidentalis* 'Rheingold' with its soft, feathery foliage, tinted old-gold in summer, turning copper-gold in winter; one that does considerably change its appearance during the year, and all the more valuable for that; it will reach a height and width of about 90 cm (3 ft) after ten years. *T. orientalis* 'Aurea Nana' is smaller still, a rounded little shrub never more than 60 cm (2 ft) high, with bright yellow-tipped foliage. Also good for golden foliage is *Chamaecyparis lawsoniana* 'Minima Aurea', bright yellow all year and tiny enough for the smallest rock garden. Taller than these, making a thin column of golden-tipped foliage no more than 1 m (4 ft) high after ten years, *C. lawsoniana* 'Ellwood's Gold' is excellent for adding height and scale at the back of a rock garden or raised rock bed.

Chamaecyparis pisifera 'Boulevard' is a popular choice, and rightly so, for its intense silvery-blue foliage, forming a bushy little tree that is wonderfully soft to the touch, and only about 90 cm (3 ft) tall after ten years. Equally popular, and a good one for the rock garden, is *Picea glauca* 'Albertiana Conica'; the very best of the conical conifers, it is perfectly shaped and a marvellously fresh pale green in spring and summer; its growth is a little slower than 'Boulevard'.

Neat as some of these are, the most perfect dwarf conifer for growing with alpines is the tiny *Juniperus communis* 'Compressa'. This is a very slow-growing and diminutive tree with the lovely spire-shape of the full-sized junipers, yet unlikely to reach more than 60 cm (2 ft) in a lifetime; it is one of the best for creating a 'miniature landscape' look in a small rock garden or in an alpine trough or sink garden. Some of the tiniest bun-shaped or hedgehog-like dwarf conifers are equally slow-growing as far as height is concerned, but are inclined to spread sideways—a point to bear in mind when planting with rock plants. One of the best of these is the bird's nest spruce, *Picea abies* 'Nidiformis', which makes a spreading flat-topped bush, usually with a nest-like hollow in the top.

Some of the more vigorous prostrate ground-covering conifers spread far and wide, becoming a nuisance in a small garden, and cutting them back hard only results in an ugly mess of bare wood. The spreading junipers, *Juniperus horizontalis* varieties, are probably the worst offenders,

some of them making mats more than 2 m (7 ft) across in under ten years.

Juniperus procumbens 'Nana' is slower, usually only growing to about 90 cm or 1.25 m (3 or 4 ft) across in ten years; this is sometimes sold as *J.* 'Bonin Isles' and is very prostrate, a pleasant apple-green in colour. One of the most colourful, and not too fast-spreading, is *J. communis* 'Depressa Aurea'; its spring foliage is a bright yellow, turning golden and then green-yellow as summer progresses, finally becoming bronze-tinted in winter.

6
Hardy Perennial Plants

Perennials for spring

It is difficult to say exactly when winter ends in the garden and spring begins; so many early plants and bulbs start their display while there is still snow on the ground and a sharp frost in the air, yet are still there flowering away when it is 'woolly jumpers off, and let's get out in the sunshine' time. And probably the very best of these winter–spring plants for the small garden are the primroses. Few other plants can rival them for their long flowering period, neatness and ease of growth, hardiness and sheer beauty and charm—and all at a time of year when most garden plants are afraid even to raise their sleepy heads out of the cold soil.

That trusty old primrose 'Wanda' is a good example. Its first claret-red blooms start to appear, come snow or arctic freeze-up, in January and February, gradually increasing in number and building up to a crescendo in April, when the neat and glossy dark green leaves literally disappear beneath a sea of short-stemmed flowers which last well into May. Not satisfied with that, 'Wanda' will continue to push up a few flowers throughout summer, and often still have energy left over to put on a minor display in autumn.

The wild primrose, too, should be in every small garden; not, of course, as plants filched from the countryside (where they are becoming rarer every year) but nursery-bought or quickly and easily raised from seed. Indeed, there can be few more evocative sights in the spring garden than a drift of delicate yellow primrose blooms shining palely out from under a shrub or the base of a hedge in March and April.

And there are many more lovely primroses to be sought out in catalogues and nurseries: the superb double forms, yellow, white and lilac; old single varieties like the pink-flowered and bronze-leaved 'Garryarde Guinevere'; the crimson 'Gloria'; 'Blue Riband' (a marvellous deep sky-blue); and the stunning appleblossom-pink *sibthorpii* which blooms over the same long period as 'Wanda', the two of them making perfect companion plants. These are but a tiny sample of the old varieties, of which there were once scores; and it is surprising how many you can still find if you are prepared to hunt for them.

Most of the old varieties are hybrids raised from the purple-red-flowered East European primrose *Primula juliae* (somewhat mixed with blood from our own wild primrose and the pink-flowered species *sibthorpii*) which was the parent of 'Wanda'; and they can generally be found in hardy plant catalogues (especially alpine catalogues) listed as *juliae*, 'Juliana' or 'Pruhonica' primroses.

All are superb for early colour and as neat as you could wish any plant to be; perfect for under-planting shady ground beneath shrubs and trees, where they mix well with small spring bulbs like crocus, chionodoxas, scillas and snowdrops; in fact, in a small garden where shade is a problem, primroses are the answer for spring—they simply cannot get too much. And those mentioned are all far more elegant than the huge-flowered modern strains of primroses so frequently seen these days, giant-flowered plants that bear little resemblance to the dainty wild flowers from which they derive. Even if you can only locate 'Wanda' and the wild primrose, I would rather see these in gardens than the 'bedding primroses'.

All the primroses demand is some humus in the soil where conditions are dry or very clayey (i.e. some peat or compost) and regular division into smaller pieces when they make large clumps —although the wild primrose, unlike the hybrids, is best left alone and undivided (increase it by seed instead). But they do benefit from a spring feed of Blood, Fish and Bone fertiliser, and a top-dressing with peat or compost if you have some to spare in spring.

Polyanthus, too, are good for early colour; but here again I would implore you to seek out neat and elegant-flowered plants in preference to the giant modern strains. There are 'old-fashioned' polyanthus around if you keep an eye out for them—smaller-flowered yellows, and enchanting Elizabethan-style silver-laced and gold-laced polyanthus. You can even find them in some local garden centres, now that they are coming back into fashion after so many unfortunate years of 'big flowers are best'.

The hellebores, yet another group of classic winter–spring flowers, are perfect for interplanting with the primroses. I shall leave the Christmas Rose, *Helleborus niger*, the earliest of all, until we come back round to midwinter; but there are still plenty of others to occupy us in late winter and early spring.

The lenten roses, the forms and varieties of *H. orientalis*, are the most important; strong, tough plants with more-or-less evergreen leaves which are a handsome sight at all times of the year, being large, glossy and deeply cut—roughly hand-shaped. The flowers are long-lasting and quite exotic for this time of year—elegantly nodding cups or chalices of pink, crimson-red, wine-purple, cream or white, frequently heavily speckled with maroon-red or crimson.

H. 'Atrorubens' is generally the first of this group to bloom, sometimes as early as January; a wonderful deep plum-red, well worth seeking out. The rest, mainly sold in colour strains of red, pink, white, etc., usually start to come into flower in February, continuing throughout March and into early May.

The wild primrose, Primula vulgaris; *a delight under trees, shrubs and hedges, or in a wild corner of the garden.*

The green-flowered hellebores are equally prized by keen gardeners. *H. corsicus* is the best of all, producing its large pale-green cup-flowers very early, above superb prickly-toothed greyish leaves. *H. foetidus*, a rare British native, almost rivals this with its large clusters of apple-green bell-flowers in late winter and spring, carried above dark evergreen foliage.

All the hellebores are as happy in shade as the primroses. Like the primroses, too, they will even tolerate dry shade beneath trees and tall shrubs, although in such a position they will benefit from some peat or compost at planting time, and an occasional top-dressing with this kind of humus-adding material will help them to give of their best. Yet they will also thrive in full sun; very accommodating plants indeed.

Many spring plants, in fact, will tolerate dry shade beneath trees and shrubs, which is very handy in a small garden. So many of them are by nature plants of woodland glades or the outskirts of woods and forests where, in the wild, they have adapted to making fast growth and flowering before the spring leaf canopy unfolds overhead, cutting off both light and summer rain.

A perfect example of this is to be found in our native wood anemone, *Anemone nemorosa*. This is a lovely little plant for the spring garden, pushing up its gleaming white wind-flowers from late March to May and then dying down completely as summer approaches, making it ideal for underplanting trees and shrubs. Roots can be bought quite cheaply from bulb nurseries, and there are also some lovely blue forms available, as well as a charming double white. Of the blues, the strongest grower is the variety 'Allenii'. You will also find *A. ranunculoides* in some bulb catalogues, a bright buttercup-yellow wood anemone but rather scarcer and therefore pricier.

Ferns are an obvious choice for shady areas, and one of the most desirable is the maidenhair-like *Adiantum pedatum* 'Japonicum', fantastic in spring when the new fronds unfurl a warm rose-bronze colour, slowly maturing to a lacy green. It is far from invasive, only slowly making a 30 cm (1 ft)-wide clump. Few other plants can rival the ferns for beauty of foliage, and one or two are an asset in any garden. Even our native hart's tongue, *Asplenium scolopendrium*, is an extremely attractive evergreen foliage plant. Again, I must reiterate, such plants should always be bought from a nursery, not collected from the wild.

Lily of the valley is a little invasive in the border, but in a patch of dry, shady soil it behaves itself better, and I would not like to forego the pleasure of picking a few of its scented flower spikes every spring. And another good plant for brightening up a dry, shady corner is E. A. Bowles' golden grass, *Milium effusum* 'Aureum': bright golden-yellow leaves and airy straw-coloured flowering spikes in spring.

Bergenias, too, thrive in dry soils and shade, their large 'elephant's-ear' leaves making good ground-cover and often assuming rich winter tints of scarlet, purple-red or crimson. All are spring-flowering, either pink, crimson or white, and one of the best is the free-flowering purplish-pink *B. cordifolia* 'Purpurea', with leaves that turn purple-tinged in winter.

Rather classier and more elegant ground-cover for dry shade is provided by the dainty spring-flowering epimediums. All are evergreen, or at least retain their old leaves throughout winter, these turning handsome shades of yellow, red and bronze; in the spring, the new leaves also exhibit tinges of pink or red, while the small columbine-like flowers are produced in airy sprays, often before the leaves appear. *E. rubrum* is excellent, with young foliage strongly tinted bronze-red, and sprays of crimson flowers in May; the leaves turning orange and yellow in autumn. *E. grandiflorum* has pink or white flowers, while *E. perralderianum* is a reliably evergreen species with bright yellow sprays.

The shooting stars, the pink cyclamen-flowered dodecatheon species from North America, enjoy both shade and sun, and they are good under trees and large shrubs; they die down in any case during early summer, having a very short spring growing period, like the wood anemone. *D. meadia* is readily available and one of the showiest, with foot-high stems and a mass of rose-pink flowers.

Pulsatilla vulgaris, the pasque flower, is a spring gem, always popular for its large, silky mauve goblet-flowers and ferny leaves. There are ruby-red and white flowered forms around, but they are generally raised from seed and can vary considerably, sometimes proving very disappointing; best to see them in the nursery and pick out good forms. This plant needs good drainage and is happiest in a rock garden or raised bed where the soil is heavy; but in such a situation it also appreciates some peat to help keep the roots moist in summer.

Now to some of the most glorious flowers of spring, the paeonies. The double varieties are so widely-planted and popular that they hardly need any introduction from me, but less well-known are the elegant and rather neater single-flowered species and varieties, a little more fleeting in bloom than the doubles, but stunning in their ephemeral beauty. In many cases the young shoots are coloured deep red or bronze and the dying autumn foliage is tinted orange or yellow.

Paeonia mlokosewitschii is the tongue-twisting name by which we know one of the very loveliest of all paeonies, a slow-growing plant with handsome greyish leaves and huge bowl-shaped lemon-yellow flowers of perfect form and refinement. For sheer beauty this is only rivalled by the crystalline white *P. obovata alba*. And there are many more single-flowered species and varieties, some luscious pinks, others deep smouldering reds, and one or two snowy-whites; all superlative garden plants and well worth snapping up when you come across them. All are happy in sun or semi-shade and are good under trees or large shrubs.

Another stunner for spring is the double-flowered American bloodroot, *Sanguinaria canadensis* 'Flore Pleno', which gets its common name from the red blood-like sap that oozes from the fleshy roots when they are cut or broken. This is another woodlander that dies away as summer progresses and is therefore good under trees or tall shrubs in dry shade and also in sun.

The fully-double, gleaming white flowers appear on short stalks above bare soil in late April and are the focal-point of the garden for a week or so until wind or rain batters the petals to the

Helleborus orientalis: a good seedling with creamy-white, maroon-speckled flowers.

ground like a miniature snowstorm. The large greyish leaves follow and are good to see until midsummer, when they usually start to die down. A well-drained position is essential, with some peat mixed into the soil, preferably tucked under a shrub or small tree. Rather a scarce plant, this one, so find a nursery where they grow it, and if necessary put your name on the waiting list.

Also from North America, and again shade-tolerant woodlanders, the trilliums or wood lilies are really classy spring-flowering plants. The name trillium refers to the tripartite formation of the plants' major parts; i.e. three leaves to a stem and three petals to a flower. The best is *Trillium grandiflorum*, commonly known as the wake robin, with brilliant white, rather lily-like flowers on foot-high stems. This is fairly uncommon in gardens yet easily obtained from alpine nurserymen. Plant where it will get some shade during the day, with plenty of peat mixed into the soil; again, like so many spring plants, it is good under trees and shrubs.

Early summer perennials

Moving on into late spring and early summer, one of the plants that I remember most vividly from childhood is the lovely rose-red bleeding heart or lady's locket, *Dicentra spectabilis*, which makes such an eye-catching display in the mild weather of May and June.

The dicentra makes its best showing in a corner with some shade, where the deeply-divided foliage will grow luxuriantly and provide an interesting feature until it starts to die down again in midsummer; the short growing season making this another good plant for placing right in amongst summer-flowering plants which will fill the gap and give double value from the same patch of ground.

Violets are superb for colour in spring and early summer. All are dainty little plants, and you will find an excellent range in alpine nurserymen's lists—blues, whites and bright yellows. One of the very best for general planting in sunny or semi-shaded beds is *Viola cornuta*, a strong-growing plant which smothers itself with rich violet-blue flowers in June and July; and if you keep it watered, it will continue pushing up a few

blooms throughout the summer. I particularly like the neat *V. cornuta* 'Minor', with paler lavender-blue flowers, suitable for the rock garden; and the magnificent white form, probably the longest-flowering of all, producing its snowy blooms abundantly in May, June and July, then sporadically right through to summer's end—provided it is not allowed to get too dry at the roots.

But the most important plants of all for this transitional period from late spring to early summer are the irises, surely the most shapely and classically beautiful of all garden flowers, and so wonderfully varied in their size, colour range and suitability for different situations in the garden. The stiff sword-leaves of all but the coarsest flag irises also make a good contrast to plants of a more soft and bushy nature.

The *Iris sibirica* varieties are probably the best all-round garden plants, easily grown in moist or dry soils; however, in a very dry and sunny border they do best with some peat, and with plenty of water around flowering time. The leaves are grassy, much more elegant than those of the tall bearded iris hybrids, and the flowers are rather neater yet very showy. Named varieties include the well-named 'Heavenly Blue', the purple-flowered 'Caesar' and the white 'Snow Queen'.

Lovelier still is *I. hoogiana*, one of the most stunning of all the irises with its large fragrant lavender-blue blooms of a unique satiny texture; always available from the bulb firm of Van Tubergen, but not widely offered elsewhere, this is one for a sunny corner.

Those mentioned so far are fairly tall plants, but there are also plenty of smaller irises, some of them suitable for the rock garden as well as the front of a border or a raised bed. My first choice would be the Californian species *innominata*, *douglasiana* and *tenax*. The hybrids between these, known as 'Californian Hybrids' or 'Pacific Coast Hybrids', are more commonly seen in gardens and catalogues, but the species are worth

Adiantum pedatum, *a superb little fern for the small garden; this is the form 'Japonicum', which produces wonderful rosy-brown young fronds in spring.*

seeking out. The hybrids range in height from 23–45 cm (9–18 ins) and in colour from white through palest blue, lavender and pink to deep purples; from creamy yellows to orange-buff. Some are better than others, the pastel shades and pale yellows being the most attractive; when only a mixed seed-raised strain is on offer, it is best to select good plants in flower.

A lime-free soil is essential for the Californian irises, but all will succeed if planted in peat beds or pockets of a peaty mixture where the garden is limy. Although best in semi-shade, they will tolerate full sun if given plenty of peat and kept watered around flowering time; they are good in raised beds.

Other neat irises include the violet-blue *graminea*, which smells mouth-wateringly like stewed plums, the free-flowering blue or purple-blue *setosa*, the drought-loving lilac *tectorum*, and the very dwarf purple-blue *ruthenica*.

Candelabra primulas are classic plants for early summer, the name referring, of course, to the way the flowers are carried in branching whorls up the length of the stem. *Primula japonica* is free-flowering, the named varieties 'Millar's Crimson' and 'Postford White' being particularly striking. *P. pulverulenta* is similar but more elegant, with rich crimson-purple flowers. I also like the giant Himalayan cowslip, *P. sikkimensis*, delightfully fragrant in June and July when its heads of lemon-yellow flowers burst open atop 45 cm (18 ins) stems. Although tall, these primulas do not take up a great deal of room and are quite happy in light shade, preferably with plenty of peat. They look very good under trees or tall shrubs, but may need some heavy watering in spring and summer where the soil dries out.

Meconopsis betonicifolia, the blue Himalayan poppy, flowers with the primulas in June and July and goes superbly with the pale yellow *Primula sikkimensis*, enjoying the same moist and semi-shaded conditions. Unfortunately, the large sky-blue poppy flowers turn a duller lilac-blue or even mauve on limy soils, and in this situation the meconopsis should be planted on a peat bed or in a large pocket of peaty mixture in a shady border, as I have to do. There are other blue meconopsis, but few that can rival this one for purity of colour;

the exception is *M. grandis* 'G.S. 600', which is sometimes available—at a high price—and produces large shapely flowers of a very rich blue.

The foxtail lilies, the eremurus species and hybrids, may seem rather large plants for a small garden, with their long, broad, flopping sword-leaves; but even if you can just squeeze in one plant, it will make a great summer feature. And since the foliage dies away almost as the plants flower in early summer, you can plant bushy things like geraniums or penstemons closely around the eremurus to take advantage of the gap that is left (taking care not to damage the wide-spreading fleshy roots of the eremurus). Most produce thick red-hot-poker-like flower stems up to 2 m (6 ft) tall, the top half of each stem a mass of delicate starry flowers for anything up to a month —a real Roman Candle effect. I grow the pink-flowered *Eremurus robustus* which, on deep soil, may top 2.5 m (8 ft) with its flowering stem; and in my very dry garden it still achieves an impressive 2 m (6 ft).

Also exotic, if on a smaller scale, are the pink trumpet-flowered incarvilleas. Best-known is *Incarvillea delavayi* which produces its rose-red trumpets on 60 cm (2 ft) stems in June, above good-looking deeply-cut foliage, a fine plant for well-drained soil in full sun. Neater, at just 30 cm (1 ft) tall, but with equally large pink trumpets, is *I. mairei*, while its dwarf forms, 'Frank Ludlow' and 'Nyoto Sama', are just 15 cm (6 ins) tall, still with large trumpet-flowers.

Aquilegias, or columbines, are popular for early summer, and I like the blue *alpina*; this is a neat plant, quite happy to have its ferny grey-green leaves and 60 cm (2 ft) flower stems scrambling up through other things, easy to please in either sun or shade. The foliage develops quite late, making this a good plant to mix with clumps of spring bulbs, where it will fill the gap when the bulb leaves die down.

Perennials all summer long
The plants discussed in the following pages will flower freely over a long period from early summer onwards, providing weeks or even months of non-stop colour. These, or at least some of them, should form the backbone of the summer garden,

Brightness for the dark days of the year. Right:
The lime-tolerant heather, Erica mediterranea
'Brightness', flowering in March. Below:
Snowdrops in late winter, with the handsome
flaking bark of Acer griseum *and the attractive*
foliage of Cyclamen hederifolium *and*
Helleborus orientalis; *a delightful woodland*
scene created in a small corner.

Top left: A small summer rock garden; main splashes of colour from Campanula garganica *and* Hypericum olympicum *grown as edging plants. Rock gardens in miniature can be created in home-made containers: left: a trough containing various forms of the alpine* Primula marginata *with a dwarf box tree,* Buxus sempervirens *'Suffruticosa'; above: tub in early summer with* Armeria caespitosa *'Bevan's Variety',* Campanula fenestrellata, *dwarf geraniums and a* Dianthus allwoodii *seedling (in side planting hole).*

Neat plants for small rock gardens. Top left :
Dianthus alpinus; *top right : the spring-flowering*
Gentiana verna; *bottom left : the succulent-leaved*
hybrid Lewisia *'Pinkie', from a North American*

desert species requiring very gritty soil ; bottom right :
Campanula *'Joe Elliott', a stunning hybrid named*
after its raiser, a well-known alpine nurseryman (now
retired).

Making use of walls and fences. Above: Clematis montana, *a rampant grower, making a breathtaking* display in late May; below: Roses and Jasminum officinale *around the windows in a small courtyard garden.*

along with the long-flowering shrubs discussed in the last chapter. For a start, the geraniums would certainly leave a dreadful gap if they were all suddenly and mysteriously to vanish from our summer gardens; many are rather large and floppily spreading for very small gardens, but there are also plenty of neater kinds to suit our needs.

My all-time favourite is *Geranium sanguineum*, one of the longest-flowering of all the summer plants, managing to conjure up an endless succession of candy-pink or rose-crimson blooms from late May through to autumn; all carried above low-growing and elegant lacy leaves. Mine are seedlings from a plant bought from that marvellous Scottish alpine nursery, Jack Drake's of Aviemore, and I have never had a disappointing one out of the whole bunch; all are extremely variable in colour, from pale to deep pink, but always fairly neat ground-carpeters, quite happy running about and through other plants yet never strong or tall enough to smother anything (although they can be a bit of a nuisance in the rock garden unless relegated to a corner on their own). They revel in the driest, sunniest borders and look especially fine tumbling down from the top of a retaining wall.

Rather larger, but still neat as geraniums go, is the hybrid 'Johnson's Blue', making a 30 cm (1 ft) high clump of divided leaves with a spread of about 60 cm (2 ft), covered from June to August with pure-blue flowers—an absolute sensation in full sun or semi-shade. *G. endressii* 'Wargrave Pink' and *G. wallichianum* 'Buxton's Blue' also flower all summer, the first a good bright pink and the second clear blue with a contrasting white centre; these are more wide-spreading, eventually making clumps up to 90 cm (3 ft) across, but easy in sun or shade where there is room for them. The very neatest geraniums suitable for rock gardens will be discussed in Chapter Seven.

Many of the campanulas, both the tall border bellflowers and the smaller rock plants, bloom over an equally long period, starting in June and continuing through to August.

The most elegant and neat of the taller sorts is *Campanula persicifolia*; the name means peach-leaved, and the long, thin leaves are attractive all year round, making a solid evergreen clump up to 30 cm (1 ft) wide. The cup-shaped blue flowers are carried on stiff 90 cm (3 ft) stems that never need any staking (unlike so many tall campanulas) and are produced non-stop from June to late August or even September. It is suitable for sun or shade. The ordinary species is extremely good, but there is also a larger-flowered variety, 'Telham Beauty', and a very pretty white which looks good in deep shade.

C. carpatica is a rock plant that is usually a little too tall and vigorous to look right in the rock garden, but it is superb towards the front of a border or as an edging plant. The large saucer-flowers are held facing the sky on stalks of about 30 cm (1 ft) in height, so that the full beauty of the flowers is easily seen and admired. Many named varieties are available in various shades of china-blue, deep indigo-blue and violet-blue, as well as glistening white—all marvellous for a long display and content with a dry soil in full sun. As in the case of the geraniums, the more dwarf campanulas will be mentioned in the chapter on rock plants.

Oenothera missouriensis is a ground-hugging shrubby evening primrose that is excellent for the border-front and a good companion plant for *Campanula carpatica*, enjoying the same dry, sunny conditions. The lemon-yellow flowers are huge, up to 10 cm (4 ins) across, produced for weeks on end. Never more than a few inches off the ground, the branching shoots spread to make a mat 60 cm (2 ft) wide.

The day lilies are tough things for a dry, sunny border, where their arching pale-green grassy leaves look good sprouting up from amongst bushier, more spreading plants. The large lily-like trumpets only last individually for a day, but as one bloom dies, there's always another bursting its bud, providing a long succession of bright colour. Innumerable varieties are available in a wide colour range, but the yellows are by far the most attractive and eye-catching; the deeper the colour, the more subdued and the less effective they become; the paler yellows also tend to be more or less delicately scented, while most of the other colours lack this valuable attribute.

I would recommend 'Whichford', a free-flowering primrose-yellow, 'Marion Vaughn', lemon-yellow, and 'Golden Chimes', a fairly dwarf variety producing masses of deep yellow blooms with mahogany backs to the trumpets. 'Pink Damask' is the nearest to a clear rose-pink.

Good as the more delicately-coloured hybrids are, I would also recommend seeking out some of the elegant hemerocallis species from which they have been raised: *H. flava* (previously known by the more appropriately attractive name of *H. lilio-asphodelus*), a deliciously fragrant yellow flower of a superlative trumpet-lily shape, or *H. dumortieri*, low-growing, with deep yellow flowers, backed with mahogany-brown like 'Golden Chimes'; both bloom from late spring to early summer.

Modern pinks, the single- and double-flowered *Dianthus* 'Allwoodii' types, are also valuable for a long succession of colour at the front of the border, where their silvery-grey evergreen foliage provides handsome year-round ground-cover. Many are, of course, also highly fragrant. The variety 'Doris' is a warm rose-pink double, 'Diane' is a deeper rose-red, and 'Daphne' is a good single pink with a darker eye. All need well-drained soil and a sunny border; on heavy clay, mix in plenty of sharp or coarse sand and some peat or compost.

The blue-flowered flax, *Linum narbonnense*, is also keen on a hot, sunny situation, revelling in dry soils and flowering through the worst summer droughts. The wide-open funnel-shaped blooms are a brilliant sky-blue, produced week after week from early summer onwards, sometimes right through to autumn. A shrubby little upright plant, it is semi-evergreen in mild areas.

Penstemons are marvellous for long-lasting bright colour, but only a few are reliably hardy. One of the toughest is *P. barbartus*, with tubular foxglove-shaped flowers of a very cheery pink or rosy-scarlet, in 90 cm (3 ft) branching spikes from June to August. *P. ovatus* is another favourite of mine, reasonably hardy with me in a sunny spot on well-drained soil, and entrancing in June and July when the 45 cm (18 in) flower stems explode in a froth of sky-blue; the leaves are broad and form a neat evergreen basal clump. *P. pinifolius* is a very neat shrubby thing with feathery foliage,

seldom more than a few inches high in flower and often treated as a rock garden plant; however, it does well towards the front of a sunny border on well-drained or dry soil, where its unusual spikes of tubular orange-red blooms make a striking feature from June to September.

The hostas, or plantain lilies, have become immensely popular in recent years as summer foliage plants. All are excellent for shady borders and are happy even in the dry shade beneath trees and shrubs, where their large handsome leaves provide good ground-cover during the summer months; although here they are best given plenty of peat or compost when planting and as an occasional mulch. When planted in more open and sunny positions they demand a soil even more retentive of summer moisture, and the peat should be used lavishly.

The various species and their varieties all produce attractive shoots in spring which open out into weed-suppressing mounds of large ribbed leaves, sometimes variegated with cream, yellow or silvery-white. *H. fortunei* 'Aureo-marginata' is one of the best variegated ones, its grey-green leaves being edged with golden-yellow, retaining this colouring throughout summer; and, although this leaf effect is the main attraction, handsome spikes of pale lilac flowers are produced in July. Many of the plain-leaved species and varieties are, however, equally good for the size and form of their leaves alone, plus their elegant, sometimes scented, flowers; and many push up their flower spikes in late summer, adding valuable interest in this difficult season. One of the loveliest is the green-leaved hybrid 'Honeybells', which usually blooms in August and early September, deep mauve and fragrant.

I should also like to mention briefly here a summer-flowering plant which, while not as long in bloom as some of the plants suggested, is a real star that deserves to be more widely known: the yellow orchid-flowered *Roscoea cautleoides*. The resemblance to an orchid really is very close, although in actual fact this is a cousin of the

Sanguinaria canadensis 'Flore Pleno', the double form of the American bloodroot, in April; the large leaves appear later.

83

ginger; the delicate, hooded, pale-yellow blooms are carried on stems 30 cm (1 ft) high above orchid-like leaves, in late June or July, and are a picture of elegance and refinement. Alpine nurseries stock this, although it is not really suitable for a small rock garden, and the fleshy roots should be planted 12 or 15 cm (5 or 6 ins) deep with plenty of peat or compost mixed into the soil, in either sun or partial shade. The shoots appear very late, in June, so take care not to damage them when weeding.

Autumn-flowering perennials
Two excellent groups of late-flowering plants for the second half of summer and early autumn are the agapanthus and the crocosmias, both preferring well-drained soils and sunny borders.

Not all the agapanthus, or blue African lilies, are hardy except in our mildest southern coastal counties. But the widely-available 'Headbourne Hybrids' are all tough plants suitable even for a sunny corner in northern gardens; funnel-shaped flowers of varying shades of blue are carried from July to September, in large bunches atop stems of 60 to 90 cm (2 to 3 ft) above handsome strap-like leaves. Mine came through the winter of 1984–85 completely unharmed in a bed close to a sunny south wall.

Of the crocosmias, I like best the species *Crocosmia masonorum*, a delightful thing with its cool green sword-leaves and its arching spikes of intense orange-red flowers; the shapely blooms gradually open up the length of the flower stem over a very long period from July through to September, or sometimes even later. The hybrids, popularly known as montbretias, are rather less elegant and dainty but offer the same useful attributes of handsome foliage, attractively arching flower spikes, and a long, late season of bright colour from late summer to early autumn. They can be planted as dried corms in early spring, or as pot-grown plants later in the year, and they benefit from a heavy watering if the ground should be dry as the leaves come up in late spring. The best varieties include the flame-red 'Lucifer', the orange-red 'Bressingham Blaze', and the very late-flowering deep orange 'Emily McKenzie'.

For even later autumn colour, the tall-growing anemones are good. *Anemone hybrida* is the correct name for those popular plants sold as *Anemone japonica*, all growing to around 90 cm to 1.25 m (3 to 4 ft) with large white or pink single or semi-double flowers, produced from August to October. Even the leaves are good to look at, being large and deeply lobed. 'White Queen' is marvellous, as is the shorter-growing pink 'September Charm'. In dry gardens these are best planted in semi-shade with plenty of peat in the soil. They take a full year to settle down properly.

The hardy fuchsias discussed in the last chapter as small deciduous shrubs for late summer and autumn can just as easily be considered as herbaceous plants, since in all but the warmest counties they die back completely in winter and must be cut down in spring. Whether you think of them as shrubs or border plants, they are wonderful at this time of year.

Last of my autumn flowers are the schizostylis. These need a sunny position but enjoy moist soil; for the best flowering results, water heavily from time to time during summer. All have sword-like leaves and 60 cm (2 ft) spikes of large cup-shaped or starry flowers from September to November. *Schizostylis coccinea* 'Major' is particularly large-flowered and bright scarlet-red, 'Viscountess Byng' is the latest to bloom, free flowering and pale pink, and 'Sunrise' is a large-flowered early pink.

Perennials for winter flowers
I have already discussed some of the best plants for late winter and early spring; those mentioned below are among the earliest to flower. *Helleborus niger*, the ever-popular Christmas rose, is best in shade and in a sheltered spot, ideally under a shrub that will protect its gleaming white midwinter blooms from the batterings of rain, snow and sharp frosts. It seldom actually flowers for Christmas, but makes a nice show from January to March. Plant with plenty of peat or compost and it will make a fine mound of handsome divided grey-green foliage. One or two named

Viola cornuta alba: *a stunning little violet, flowering all summer long.*

forms, selected for their outstanding blooms, are around and worth paying extra for; e.g. *H. niger* 'Potter's Wheel'.

The other classic winter flower is the low-growing evergreen *Iris unguicularis* (still better known under its older and lovelier name of *I. stylosa*). The blooms are exquisitely formed, varying from palest lavender-blue to deeper purple-blues. Flowering time also varies considerably, depending on the individual plant and how much of a baking it received during the preceding summer; moreover, new plants usually take quite some time to settle down and start flowering at all. This Algerian native is adapted to an arid climate, so is best grown tucked up hard against the base of a sunny wall in poor, stony soil. Do not feed with nitrogenous fertilisers, just with a sprinkling of sulphate of potash in the spring. 'Walter Butt' is a good lilac-blue form, and 'Mary Barnard' a deeper blue.

7
Rock Plants

When it comes to rock plants, the well-known stronger types are of course suitable not only for rockeries, but for the fronts of borders as well, and many are perfect for trailing down retaining walls; such things as the spring-flowering violet, blue, pink and red aubrietas and the yellow *Alyssum saxatile*, the summer-flowering pink or red thrift, *Armeria maritima*, and the ground-hugging shrubby rock roses (the helianthemum varieties).

These kinds of plants make good evergreen ground-cover for dry sunny borders and banks, and the helianthemums in particular are superb for a non-stop show of colour throughout the summer. However, they are too rampant for very small rock gardens or raised beds, where they tend to swamp smaller and more precious things. If they are used for a quick effect in a new rock garden or raised bed, keep them tucked into corners or around the edges where they can spill downwards and outwards without causing so much trouble—and remove them the minute they start to become a nuisance.

The plants I shall be recommending are mostly neater things, few of which will outgrow even the tiniest rock garden or raised bed. In fact, many are neat enough for planting in miniature sink and trough gardens; a lovely way to grow these dainty alpines.

What rock plants need above all is a well-drained soil, which means a bed or border raised up several centimetres at least, and preferably 30 cm (1 ft) or more, above the general garden level, and with plenty of grit, sharp sand and peat added. A raised bed supported by a low retaining wall is ideal; but even a slightly raised border sloping up towards the back will do, and there need not even be any rock in it (although a few rocks do add immeasurably to the effect).

The site should be open and reasonably sunny, and it should never be overhung by trees, tall shrubs or house gutters which may drip onto the alpines during winter. Nor should alpines be over-fed; they do best with just a scattering of a long-lasting and slow-release fertiliser like John Innes Base applied in spring—only a thin dusting over the soil around the plants. Top-dressing the soil of the alpine bed or rock garden with gravel looks effective and natural, and it also helps to keep the roots cool and moist in summer while protecting the flowers and foliage from soil-splashing; tuck the gravel right under each plant, to help keep the leaves off the damp soil.

Some of the tougher, mat-forming alpines are also suitable for planting in the crevices in paving, and even in gravel paths, where the traffic is not so heavy as to put them too much at risk from being trampled to death. And many look good in the crevices of a dry-stone retaining wall, or in planting holes left when building a cemented retaining wall, as discussed in Chapter Three.

Always make weeding alpine beds and rock gardens a priority, since even a few small weeds may quickly smother some of these dainty plants; in particular, watch out for weeds seeding into the centre of mat-forming plants, and get these out before they grow too large. And keep alpines well watered during dry spells in late spring and early summer as, being mountain plants, they are used to receiving ample moisture at this time from melting snowfields, and this is when many of them do most of their growing. After mid-July, all but the very late flowering plants can generally

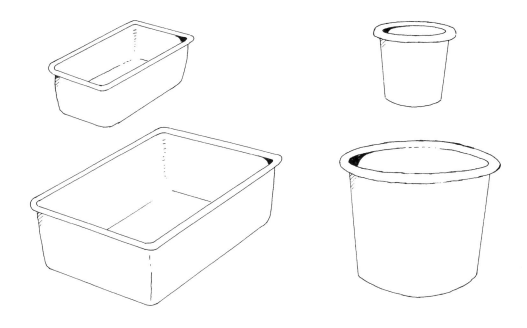

ANY CONTAINERS WHICH WILL FIT ONE
INSIDE THE OTHER WITH A 5 to 7·5 CM (2 to 3 in)
GAP BETWEEN THEM CAN BE USED
AS MOULDS TO MAKE TROUGHS AND
TUBS WITH A CEMENT-PEAT-SAND MIX.

look after themselves and will probably not need watering except in the event of severe drought.

Making a trough garden

Old stone sinks and troughs are the ideal containers for the smallest rock plants, but how scarce they are these days—and expensive, too. The next-best alternative is to make your own, using a mixture of sand, cement and peat devised by alpine enthusiasts over the years for just this purpose. First you need two wooden boxes or two plastic containers, one of which will fit inside the other with a gap of 5–7 cm between them all round. I have experimented with specially-made wooden box moulds, with the large plastic 'planters' available from garden centres, and with the largest sizes of semi-rigid plastic pots; the plastic containers make longer-lasting moulds, and the

set concrete mixture is more easily removed from these than from the rougher wooden moulds.

Whatever container you choose, your first step is to place small pots in the bottom of the larger one (5 cm or 2 in pots are about right), to support the inner box or container and leave a gap of about 7.5 cm (3 ins) between their bases. Prepare a mix of one part cement, one part sharp sand (not silver sand) and two parts peat (all measured by bulk, not weight). Add water to make a consistency that is not too sloppy or runny, but nice and firm and mouldable. The base of the outer container is filled with this mixture to the tops of the small supporting pots, giving a depth to the base of about 7.5 cm. The smaller box or container (the inner mould) is placed on the pots and the layer of concrete mixture, and then more concrete is packed into the gap all around between

MAKING A TROUGH IN A WOODEN MOULD

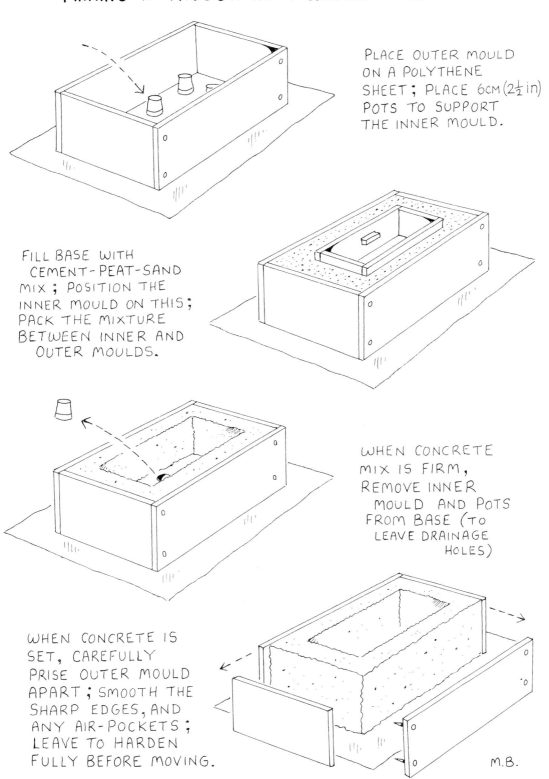

PLACE OUTER MOULD ON A POLYTHENE SHEET; PLACE 6cm (2½in) POTS TO SUPPORT THE INNER MOULD.

FILL BASE WITH CEMENT-PEAT-SAND MIX; POSITION THE INNER MOULD ON THIS; PACK THE MIXTURE BETWEEN INNER AND OUTER MOULDS.

WHEN CONCRETE MIX IS FIRM, REMOVE INNER MOULD AND POTS FROM BASE (TO LEAVE DRAINAGE HOLES)

WHEN CONCRETE IS SET, CAREFULLY PRISE OUTER MOULD APART; SMOOTH THE SHARP EDGES, AND ANY AIR-POCKETS; LEAVE TO HARDEN FULLY BEFORE MOVING.

M.B.

MAKING A WOODEN MOULD FOR CONCRETE TROUGHS

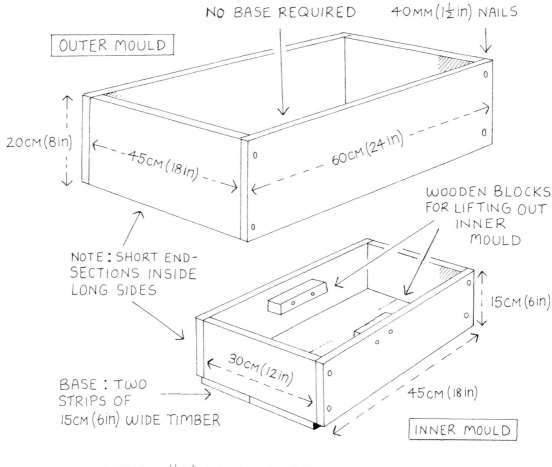

NO BASE REQUIRED

40MM (1½in) NAILS

OUTER MOULD

20CM (8in)

45CM (18in)

60CM (24in)

NOTE: SHORT END-SECTIONS INSIDE LONG SIDES

WOODEN BLOCKS FOR LIFTING OUT INNER MOULD

15CM (6in)

BASE: TWO STRIPS OF 15CM (6in) WIDE TIMBER

30CM (12in)

45CM (18in)

INNER MOULD

USE 12MM (½in) THICK TIMBER THROUGHOUT

M.B.

the two, to form the walls of the trough; continually tamp this down to eradicate air gaps.

Fill to the top of the outer mould to obtain the maximum depth possible inside the trough, to allow for plenty of room for planting and for root growth. Chicken wire can be put in the base and sides as these are filled, to reinforce the concrete mix; I do not always bother with this, but then I have been known to break the occasional trough,

so perhaps it is a good idea. Leave for a few hours until set enough for the inner mould to be gently tugged out and leave the trough walls standing up inside the outer mould. Leave like this for at least 24 hours and preferably more, until hard enough for the outer mould to be removed. With a wooden box mould, the nailed-together sides can be gently prised apart with a screwdriver to leave the trough standing free; but with a plastic container, this needs to be carefully lifted (supporting the trough inside) and turned upside down so that the trough can gently slide out onto a padded layer of cardboard or newspapers. Two people are really essential for this part. Do not try to move the trough for a further three days, since it is not yet fully hardened; and do not attempt to turn an upside-down trough from a plastic mould the right way up until fully hardened.

Before the trough does harden, you can artificially 'age' it by chipping some small lumps out of the sides and smoothing down the edges and outer surfaces with a moist cloth. At the same time, remove the small pots from the base, thus leaving you with drainage holes.

The peat in the mixture slightly darkens the tone of the finished product, so that it looks less glaringly artificial than an ordinary concrete container; use peat that is fairly dry or just moist, not wet, and sift out the larger lumps. The peat content will also encourage attractive mosses and lichens to grow on the trough, and these can be further encouraged by painting the outside, when dry, with a coating of a liquid manure such as Bio or Maxicrop.

One final tip: with the last couple of troughs that I have made, I lined the outer mould with a sheet of polythene (a dustbin liner, actually) before filling with the concrete mixture, since my plastic containers used as moulds had become rather rough; the polythene sheet made it much easier to get the troughs out; and the wrinkles in the polythene also created one or two shallow 'cracks' in the surface of the trough walls which looked very effective and natural, like weathered stone.

Stones, broken clay pots or plastic mesh should be placed over the drainage holes to stop soil falling out, and then the trough may be filled. I like to use a peat-based potting compost with plenty of additional sharp sand and grit for the extra drainage that alpines love and need; one measure of sharp sand or grit to two measures of peat potting compost is about right. A small rock, a dwarf conifer or alpine shrub, some slow-growing rock plants, and a top-dressing of grit or gravel, and you have a miniature rock garden that will give years of pleasure.

Rock plants in paving

Plants for paving should be mainly low carpeters. However, the occasional taller plant towards the edges of a paved area will provide contrast and help to break up the flatness of the slabs; preferably something narrowly upright rather than very bushy and space-hungry, like an iris, a crocosmia, or perhaps a fern for a shady spot. Dianthus are excellent, making low evergreen mats, tolerating dry conditions well and providing useful summer colour. My favourite for gravel paths and paving is the very strong-growing *Dianthus deltoides* in its deep pink and scarlet-red forms. The more rampant dwarf campanulas are also good for a splash of blue summer colour, particularly *Campanula portenschlagiana*, and the nodding bluebell-flowered *C. cochlearifolia*. *Hypericum olympicum* makes a tiny spreading bush and is superb for its long display of large yellow flowers, so good with the blue of the campanulas. Helianthemums also flower over a long period but make wide mats in time and are better towards the edges of paving, to help break up the hard line of a patio, for example.

For late spring, the spiky hummocks and pale pink flowers of the dwarf thrift, *Armeria caespitosa* are good, and so are the many varieties of the mat-forming *Phlox subulata*. The different colour forms of the common wild thyme, *Thymus serpyllum* (now correctly called *T. drucei*) make tough aromatic mats over which it is a pleasure to stroll. Pink, red and white flowered varieties are available, providing colour from June to August. And for colourful foliage, there are of course the numerous different types of fleshy-leaved sedums and sempervivums.

In these very dry situations, always make sure that the plants have some good peaty soil around their roots, and keep them well watered until thoroughly established.

Spring-flowering rock plants

Although there are plenty of rock plants for summer, there is no doubt that spring is the great alpine season; those weeks from March to May are the time when many of the daintiest and most enchanting of these mountain plants are to be seen at their best. Some of the very first to show colour, regardless of snow or frost, are the kabschia saxifrages; with their inch-high cushions of tightly-packed silvery and grey-green foliage, studded with bright button flowers of purest white, yellow, pink and red, these captivating little plants never fail to attract admiration from enthusiasts and novices alike.

They are ideal slow-growing plants for sink and trough gardens, as well as for choice spots in the rock garden or raised bed, where the first few flowers generally start to appear as early as February, slowly increasing in numbers until the cushions of foliage disappear beneath a haze of delicate blooms in March and April. All do best where they will not catch the full glare of the summer sun, such as on north or west slopes of rock gardens or beds, tucked up against the shady side of a rock, or receiving some shade during the day from a dwarf conifer or shrub. On a south-facing slope they tend to suffer from sun scorch.

Of those I grow, I like best the various white and yellow-flowered forms of *Saxifraga burseriana*, the shell-pink hybrids 'Jenkinsae' and 'Irvingii', and the deep rose-pink 'Cranbourne'; but there are dozens more to choose from in specialist catalogues, all lovely. Of those mentioned, 'Jenkinsae' is the strongest grower and one of the most free-flowering; equally strong, and quickly making a wide mat spangled with clusters of rich yellow flowers, is the variety 'Boston Spa'.

The trailing mat-forming *S. oppositifolia* is even more appreciative of a cool planting site on a slope away from the sun or behind a rock, and it likes plenty of peat. It, too, produces tiny button flowers, of a deep heather-pink or rose-red tint, a little later in the season. 'Ruth Draper' is about the best form, a rich red and more free-flowering than some.

Following closely on the heels of the early cushion saxifrages, and overlapping with the end of their flowering season, come the alpine primulas, yet another classic group of rock plants. The one that does best with me, and which has given me years of pleasure, is *Primula marginata* in its various colour forms and varieties. Luckily this is also one of the loveliest, with its handsomely toothed and silvery-powdered leaves—a joy in

themselves—quite apart from the glory of the large heads of iridescent flowers, almost true-blue in some varieties and ranging through lilac-blue and lavender to rich purple. All are marvellous, and well worth collecting for their great variety.

P. auricula is of course well-known through its many-hued florist's border flower varieties. For the rock garden, 'Blairside Yellow' is a charming miniature form, just 7.5 cm (3 ins) tall even in bloom, with deep primrose-yellow flowers. The true wild, yellow auricula is also sometimes available, not much taller and a real stunner. A range of tiny hybrids between the wild auricula and other small alpine primulas, known as the Pubescens hybrids, is also available. All are lovely, with white, cream-white, crimson-red, brick-red and violet blooms.

These constitute the most reliable and free-flowering of the alpine primulas, all good for sink gardens as well as the rock garden; but there are a great many more to be found in specialist catalogues once you get the taste for them; and, believe me, you will, once you start growing them.

Pulsatilla vulgaris, mentioned under hardy perennials for spring, is a marvel when its mauve pasque flowers open in April. The silky seed-heads look good until June, and the ferny foliage is an attribute all summer through. However, the cultivated forms of this, unlike the very dwarf rare native form of English chalk downlands, may eventually get rather large for a very small rock garden and have to be lovingly removed to a sunny border or to a spot under deciduous shrubs.

Something that will never outgrow its allotted space (though all rock gardeners no doubt wish that it would) is the dainty star gentian of spring, *Gentiana verna*. Of all the spring and summer gentians, this is the most thrilling, its flowers the truest and most wonderful intense sky-blue. When visitors spot my patches in bloom during May they seldom have eyes for anything else. The

Saxifraga burseriana *'Gloria', one of the best alpine kabschia saxifrages, flowering in a home-made trough in early March.*

form *G. verna* 'Angulosa' is the one usually offered, and this is especially good, free-flowering and large in bloom; but once you have this, it is worth looking out for 'ordinary' *verna* in nursery lists as well, for a little variety in the shades of blue.

Unfortunately the spring trumpet gentian, *G. acaulis*, is far less free with its flowers, but it is exciting when it does decide to do its thing and produce a few blue trumpets; so it is worthwhile trying a plant or two of the different forms offered by nurserymen, just in case it does well for you.

The dwarf North American phlox provide the rock gardener with yet another classic group of plants. Some are vigorous ground-carpeters that rival even the aubrietas when it comes to producing solid sheets of intense colour. *Phlox subulata* is the strongest grower, flowering during April and May in a wide colour range from white, through clear pinks and pale lavender-blues, to rich rose-reds. *P. douglasii* is a little neater and generally flowers later, from May to June, in a similar colour range. Both are excellent in paving and planted in walls, and they look good trailing down from the tops of retaining walls or over the sides of large sink-gardens.

Thrifts are usually represented in gardens by the large and hummocky *Armeria maritima*. Far neater for a small rock garden, and ideal for a trough or sink-garden, is the charming *A. caespitosa*. This makes a slow-growing mat of tight spiky-looking leaves just 5 cm (2 ins) high, ablaze with pink flower heads throughout May, and the deep rose-pink 'Bevan's Variety' that I grow is one of my favourite spring alpines.

Rock plants for summer and autumn

With the advent of hot June days, a host of violas, dwarf geraniums, miniature iris species, lewisias and dianthus all begin to make their presence felt.

I have already mentioned *Viola cornuta* in Chapter Six, for spring and summer colour in the borders, and both the neat-growing pale blue *V. cornuta* 'Minor' and the delightful white form are top-class long-flowering plants for the smallest of rock gardens; ordinary *cornuta* can, unfortunately, become a little large.

In the same chapter I also discussed some

dwarf irises, and most of these will be quite at home in rock gardens and raised beds. *Iris innominata* in its various colour forms is one that I like immensely; at present my best plant of it is a blue-flowered form raised from seed, while those usually sold are yellow or buff-yellow. But the neatest iris of all for the rock garden is the diminutive *I. cristata*, never more than 10 cm (4 ins) tall, with dainty lilac-blue flowers; and more compact still is the form *I.c. lacustris*. Both are plants for peaty soil in a special corner.

Of the exotic lewisias, the easiest to grow and the showiest are the various strains of *Lewisia cotyledon*, the best-known being the 'Sunset Strain'; a resplendent mixture of pinks, rose-reds, and apricot shades, the flowers produced in elegant sprays on branching stalks. Being succulent plants originating from the American deserts, all need extremely well-drained positions in soil lightened with peat and lots of sharp sand; they are best wedged sideways into crevices between rocks or growing in walls, where winter rainwater will not collect in their fleshy rosettes.

Aquilegia alpina, mentioned in the last chapter, may sound, from its name, like a good alpine plant, but it is too large for a very small rock garden. Better to seek one of the smaller species, of which my favourite is the 10 cm (4 ins) high *A. bertolonii*; the bright blue flowers are large for the size of the plant, almost as large as a border columbine, produced over a long period from June to July.

Encrusted saxifrages are also useful for early summer, and they make handsome foliage plants, too, with their rosettes of long, thin leaves, often heavily silvered. This silvery coating or 'encrusting' of the leaves which gives the plants their popular name is due to the rosettes secreting lime taken up from the soil by their roots; so, as you would expect, they are particularly attractive in limy gardens. All produce their white summer flowers in plumes, some quite tiny, others as much as 60 cm (2 ft) long, arching up from the ground-hugging rosettes. One of the most colourful, easy to grow and free-flowering is *Saxifraga*

The crystalline white flowers of Primula pubescens 'Harlow Car', a delightful spring-flowering rock plant.

cotyledon 'Southside Seedling', with 45 cm (18 ins) plumes of red-spotted white flowers, usually in July. *S. cochlearis* 'Minor' and *S. aizoon* 'Baldensis' are two very dwarf silvery ones suitable for troughs. All look good in rock crevices and retaining walls.

Alpine dianthus always give marvellous value for space, covering themselves in bright pink or red blooms as freely as you could wish, sometimes all summer long. For troughs and small rock gardens I would recommend the slow-growing and very neat silvery-leaved *Dianthus* 'Whitehills', small-flowered but a very bright pink; *D. alpinus*, a superb large-flowered rose-pink or red with deep green leaves ('Joan's Blood' is a particularly dark red variety); and *D.* 'la Bourbrille', blue-grey leaves and large pink blooms. *D. deltoides* (the maiden pink) in its pink, red and white varieties, is a very free-flowering but fast-spreading plant which also seeds itself about a lot; it is ideal for walls and paving, where it will be a joy from June to August, but too rampant for a small rock garden.

I also rely very heavily on geraniums and campanulas for a long display of summer colour. I have already sung the praises of *Geranium sanguineum* in Chapter Six, and this again looks good in a wall or tumbling over the edge of a raised bed; but it must be kept away from small alpines which might be swamped by its vigorous growth; for a tiny rock garden, the neater *G. sanguineum lancastriense* is better; or *G. dalmaticum*, a comparatively slow-growing species with clear pink flowers and glossy leaves that take on red and orange tints during late summer and autumn. The flowers of *G. subcaulescens* are particularly striking, deep crimson-red with a contrasting black-brown centre, and this is also rather neater than *sanguineum*. Finally, another one that I grow and admire greatly is *G. napuligerum* (formerly *G. farreri*), the neatest of all, with palest apple-blossom flowers. Sad to say, this is far less common in catalogues than it once was, but keep a look-out for it.

Alpine campanulas come in a vast range, some of them very rampant. Avoid *Campanula portenschlagiana* and *C. poscharskyana* like the plague; these are useful fast-spreading plants in a large dry-stone wall, but in the rock garden they are far too invasive. *C. cochlearifolia* is charming in paving where it runs along the narrowest crevices, throwing up its dangling harebell flowers all summer long, but it spreads a little too fast in a small rock garden.

C. garganica is a much better choice, not at all invasive, and a sheet of starry blue flowers over a very long period. I also grow *C. fenestrellata* which is similar but even neater-growing. Very dwarf forms of *C. carpatica*, such as 'Turbinata', are often available from alpine nurseries, and these are also good. Finally, something unusual and very lovely to watch out for in lists: *C.* 'Warleyensis' (*C. haylodgensis plena*). This pastel-blue double flowered campanula was one of the first alpines I ever grew when, as a schoolboy, I built my first rock garden; and it still flourishes in one of my trough-gardens.

While on the subject of blue flowers for summer, I cannot move on without a word of praise for *Lithospermum diffusum*, a prostrate-growing shrubby plant which ranks alongside *Gentiana verna* as one of the bluest flowers in the garden —and that is praise indeed. In a way, it outshines even the gentian, since it blooms over such a long period, from June to October. 'Grace Ward' and 'Heavenly Blue' are the selected varieties usually offered. Just one drawback: it is a lime-hater, and in limy areas must be grown in a very well-drained peaty mixture (plenty of sand and grit).

The golden-yellow flowers of the alpine hypericums go well with these blue-flowered plants, and there are two that I would strongly recommend for their neat habit and long season of colour.

Hypericum reptans is extremely low-growing, making a spreading mat just 7.5 cm (3 ins) high, or a trailing curtain of foliage and flowers when planted to grow down a wall. The flowers are large, up to 5 cm (2 ins) across and a very deep golden-yellow, contrasting nicely with the scarlet of the unopened buds. The flowering display is long as well as colourful, lasting from July to September; and the leaves add yet another touch of useful colour with their red-brown autumn tints.

Rather taller at about 23 cm (9 ins), but still

making a neat little bush, *H. olympicum* flowers profusely in July and August, with golden blooms that match those of *reptans* in size. This looks good all year round with its grey-green foliage, provided the long flowering shoots are trimmed back in autumn to stop it looking straggly. *H. olympicum* 'Citrinum' is a paler lemon-yellow form, less easy to get hold of but good to have as a contrast. They look best as an edging to the rock garden, and both are suitable for planting in walls and paving, and will even thrive in a gravel driveway or path.

Another good plant for a splash of yellow in summer is *Linum flavum* 'Compactum', a dwarf flax with bunches of large funnel-shaped flowers from June to August. *L.* 'Gemmel's Hybrid' is even neater and just as colourful. Unfortunately, neither seems to be very long-lived, so it is wise to take a cutting or two every now and then to keep them going. Plant in a sunny spot high up on the rock garden or raised bed, with plenty of sand in the soil.

Penstemons offer the rock gardener a long flowering season and some very cheerful bright, hot colours. I mentioned one or two as front-of-the-border plants in the last chapter and, of these, the long-flowering orange-red *Penstemon pinifolius* is superb as a rock garden edging plant or tumbling over the edge of a raised bed. The blue *P. ovatus* is a little on the tall side with its 45 cm (18 in) flower stems, but the basal leaves are low-growing and make a neat clump that does not look out of place even in a small rock garden if you put it low down or on a corner. But the neatest ones, suitable even for a trough garden, are the early-flowering *P. roezlii* and *P. rupicola*; both dwarf shrubby plants with glowing rosy-red tubular flowers.

I like a little hot colour in the rock garden in summer, and the dwarf *Mimulus cupreus* 'Whitecroft Scarlet' gives me this with a never-ending succession of orange-red blooms, like glowing coals, from the last week of May through to the autumn frosts. All it demands is a position where it gets a little shade during the day or a north-facing slope, preferably low down on the rock garden where it will not be too dry.

My last plant for summer-long flowers is an evening primrose, *Oenothera acaulis*. This is a delight from June to September, its huge white flowers (up to 7.5 cm or 3 ins across) opening wide in the evening, fading to pink and collapsing the following morning; fresh blooms appear almost every single day for months on end. The flowers are such a pure glistening white that they appear to glow as dusk falls; a delight for those gardeners who always get home from work just as so many flowers are closing for the night.

O. caespitosa is an even better plant, neater and fragrant, but it seems to be hard to obtain these days—all the plants and seeds I get of it turn out to be *O. acaulis*.

Finally a late-flowering gentian, and the easiest of all to grow: *Gentiana septemfida*. The rich blue trumpet flowers are produced from late July to the end of August; and sometimes into September on one or two of my plants. The long, trailing flowering stems spread out across the ground from a central tuft of leaves, each with a terminal cluster of flowers. Any reasonably well-drained soil will suit it, and it flowers profusely every year without fail. *G. lagodechiana* is similar but carries only one flower per stem and makes less of a show.

If only the glorious autumn-flowering Himalayan gentians were as easy to please. They must have lime-free soil, and they prefer semi-shade (except in the cooler climate of the far north and Scotland, where they will tolerate full sun). A well-drained soil is essential, yet they need plenty of summer moisture, so a free hand with the peat is called for when planting. In my limy garden I manage to grow them in large pockets of a peaty mixture on the north side of rocks and on a slope of the rock garden facing away from the sun; and they will do even better in a peat bed, with the shade of rhododendrons and suchlike to keep them cool. On a flat or poorly-drained site, they will benefit from a sheet of glass in winter to protect them from becoming too wet around their necks.

G. sino-ornata is the easiest and the best autumn gentian to start with, its upturned flaring trumpets a rich blue at the end of grassy-leaved trailing stems from September to November. But there are many more, equally luscious, to be found in alpine catalogues; *G. macauleyi* 'King-fisher', for example, is a strong hybrid with large trumpets, almost as easy to please as *sino-ornata*.

Shrubs and trees in the rock garden

Apart from the lime-hating autumn gentians, most of the autumn colour in the rock garden comes from dwarf bulbs and corms, and from tuberous plants like the hardy cyclamen; and the same applies to the winter season, except that here the winter-flowering heathers come in very useful (see below). Dwarf bulbs for autumn and winter will be covered in the next chapter, but meanwhile, I'd like to take a very brief look at rock garden shrubs and trees.

Dwarf conifers have already been discussed in Chapter Five, and so have some of the most suitable flowering shrubs; so a quick resumé is all that is needed here. The dwarf daphnes deserve special mention: *Daphne cneorum* is the perfect rock shrub, growing into a low, spreading mat

and smothered with fragrant pink flowers in late spring; the form 'Eximia' is the best, free-flowering and strong-growing; if it grows leggy, bury the bare stems and they will both root and sprout new shoots along their length. *D. retusa* and *D. tangutica* are also superb neat evergreen shrubs for associating with alpine plants.

The dwarf brooms *Cytisus kewensis* and *C. beanii* are good, as is the very dwarf *C. ardoinii*. Winter heathers, such as the neat-growing and lime-tolerant *Erica carnea* and *E. darleyensis* varieties, are invaluable for winter colour, while the summer-flowering heathers, the *Calluna vulgaris* varieties, can be utilised on lime-free soils. *Berberis stenophylla* 'Corallina Compacta' is good for its orange-yellow spring flowers. Of the conifers, I can once again highly recommend the tiny spire-shaped *Juniperus communis* 'Compressa' for even the tiniest rock gardens, alpine beds and sink gardens.

8
Hardy Bulbs, Corms and Tubers

I cannot stress too often the vital role that bulbs play in a small garden, invaluable for colour in autumn, winter and early spring, and for boosting the summer display. Most are purpose-made for filling those parched areas under trees and shrubs which might otherwise go to waste; and it is easy to cram in masses of bulbs, even in the tiniest garden, if you use them for interplanting and underplanting amongst and beneath other things, as I explained in Chapter Three.

Autumn-flowering bulbs
The main bulb season runs from September through to April. Spring is the season most usually associated with bulbs, yet there are many lovely autumn-flowering types, coming at a time of year when the garden may be as much in need of colour and interest as it is in late winter and early spring. Despite that, these end-of-the-year bulbs seldom receive as much publicity as the ubiquitous spring-flowerers and are therefore less widely planted. That seems strange, since they are available in late summer or early autumn and will often make a lovely show within a month of planting—marvellous for instant effect.

The autumn crocus are superb for this, some of them flowering almost as soon as they are in the ground. The large goblet-flowered, generally mauve-pink colchicums, often mistakenly referred to as autumn crocus, also flower very quickly after planting.

Of the true autumn crocus, the showiest is the blue-flowered *Crocus speciosus*, available in a number of named forms varying from the deepest Oxford blue of 'Oxonian' to the paler lavender-blues of 'Artabir', 'Aitchisonii' and 'Cassiope'; all are large-flowered, fast to increase and stunning in drifts or clumps beneath trees and shrubs. I like to grow little clumps of three or four corms together in the rock garden. Brilliant as the blues are, you will be depriving yourself of a treat if you do not also grow a clump of the snowy-white *C. speciosus* 'Albus', one of the very best white crocus and extremely elegant. I grow them all, since they vary somewhat in their flowering times, and a range of varieties means a longer season of colour.

C. zonatus (or *C. kotschyanus* as it is now to be called) is sold in just about every garden centre and shop during late August and September, but unfortunately most of the corms on general sale are of a very poor-flowering form which produces masses of grassy leaves with hardly ever a bloom in sight. If you want to see the delicate rosy-lilac flowers popping up all around the garden, order it from a small specialist grower who can guarantee his strain to be free-flowering; indeed, some of the smaller bulb firms make a point of this in their catalogues.

For rich lilac-purple colour in October and November, choose the strong-growing *C. medius*; a striking flower with contrasting orange-red stigmata, very dwarf and sturdy, so good on the rock garden. Just as fine is *C. goulimyi*, a recently discovered beauty from Greece—a very shapely lavender-blue, stunning, and strong-growing, too. And there are more to be found in specialist bulb catalogues: the deep purple *C. nudiflorus* and the yellow-throated pale lilac *C. pulchellus*, and . . . but then I am a bulboholic and could go on for ever. I shall leave you to discover the rest if and when (like me) you catch the crocus bug. All these bloom before, or just as, the leaves appear, their flowers spearing eye-catchingly from the bare earth.

The colchicums do the same, the large flowers pushing up leafless in September and October, the leaves only expanding the following spring; these are very large and floppy as bulb foliage goes, so they need placing with care. Under trees and shrubs is good, and in the border they are best amongst largish summer-flowering plants which will swell out and hide the untidy leaves and the gap left when these die down. But it is in autumn that they reveal their full glory. *Colchicum speciosum* and its varieties are the most elegant, like lilac-pink or rosy-red tulips; and *C. speciosum* 'Album' is one of the classiest and most beautiful flowers that any garden can boast, a huge bowl of glistening white. 'Violet Queen' is a good chequered rose-violet and 'The Giant' lives up to its name, a large mauve-pink with a white centre. Again, I could go on and on.

Some of the hardy cyclamen are, of course, extremely valuable for autumn colour. The pink *Cyclamen neapolitanum* (now correctly *C. hederifolium*) is so well known as hardly to need a description from me. Suffice it to say that it may start to flower as early as August and continue as late as November, the time varying from one tuber to another; so the more you have, the longer you will enjoy them—and who could have too many? Who, moreover, having seen the white form, would not want this as well? The silver-marbled leaves also provide attractive ground-cover through to late spring; and, as every gardening writer is quick to point out, this cyclamen will thrive under shrubs and trees, even right up to the trunk of a mature tree.

So, too, will *C. cilicium*, a dainty thing with rounded silvery leaves and paler blush-pink, very elegantly shaped flowers. Another beauty, less commonly planted, is *C. europaeum* (now renamed *C. purpurascens*), with strongly violet-scented carmine-red flowers, which puts out its display earlier, from July to September. Although these last two do well under shrubs and trees, enjoying the dry shade, a tuber or two will also look good in a not-too-hot spot in the rock garden or raised bed (preferably with a little

shade) where they can be admired at closer quarters.

The yellow autumn-flowering *Sternbergia lutea*, sometimes confusingly labelled 'autumn daffodils' by garden centres, is usually very shy-flowering, although tempting to buy. Some of the smaller specialist bulb growers offer forms which are more free-flowering than those on general sale. *S. clusiana* has larger golden-yellow flowers but needs a very well-drained soil and does not seem to last long.

Oxalis lobata is a delightful little yellow-flowered plant for a sunny, sandy spot in the rock garden or raised bed, where it blooms in September but needs the protection of a pane of glass in winter. It is unusual in that the tiny shamrock leaves appear in spring, die down for the summer, reappear at flowering time and then go to rest again for the winter. You can obtain it from specialist bulb growers.

No discussion of autumn bulbs would be complete without a mention of *Nerine bowdenii*, its iridescent pink flower clusters so lovely in September and October. Although hardy, it is best in the warmest, sunniest border available, a wall bed being ideal, where it will flower all the more profusely. It blooms best when it has been left undisturbed for a while to make crowded clumps, and enjoys a dose of sulphate of potash in spring; it also likes plenty of sand in the soil. 'Fenwick's Variety', a particularly vigorous, tall and large-flowered form originating from a Cotswold garden, is available from some smaller bulb growers.

Bulbs in winter

Crocus laevigatus 'Fontenayi' is a deliciously fragrant little flower for the dark days, lilac-blue inside, feathered violet-purple outside, which appears from late November to January. Plant it in a sunny, sheltered spot where the winter flowers will be protected from rain and snow (e.g. close to a wall). Wonderful to pick in midwinter, even a few blooms will fill a warm room with their

Galanthus 'S. Arnott', a large-flowered form of the common snowdrop, flowering through a carpet of Cyclamen hederifolium (C. neapolitanum) *leaves in January.*

honey-scent. A good subject for the rock garden.

The hardy *Cyclamen coum* should be in every garden, for its deep rose-pink and ruby-red flowers so freely produced from late December or early January through to March, making a fantastic picture when they peep up through the snow. I like to plant it with snowdrops, to get the same eye-catching contrast of red and pristine white even when there is no snow on the ground. This, like the autumn kinds, does well under shrubs and trees, and a tuber or two will also brighten up the winter rock garden. The white form is attractive but less showy, the flower marked with crimson-red at the base.

Of snowdrops for late winter and early spring I could speak volumes of praise and admiration, but I shall try to restrict myself to one or two of the best and most reliable.

Galanthus nivalis is the lovely common snowdrop, perfect for underplanting trees and shrubs, and enchanting in the roots of a hedge (along with the wild primrose). But there are also larger-flowered varieties available which, although more expensive, will make a lovely picture even as a small clump of just three bulbs—and if you choose a shady spot, prepare the soil well, feed with John Innes Base fertiliser and leave them alone, they will not stay small clumps for long; give them three years, and they should have doubled or trebled in good soil, at which time you can split them up and start again, creating new clumps.

The best time to lift and divide is while they are in growth, just after flowering, and this is also the best time to buy and plant; many small growers now sell snowdrops 'in the green'.

Galanthus 'S. Arnott' is one of the best, a beautiful large-flowered variant of the common snowdrop, as is the strong-growing *G.* 'Atkinsii'. And *G. plicatus* is a particularly giant-flowered species, originally brought to Britain by soldiers returning from the horrors of the Crimean War, where it is said that this striking flower, blooming in the bitter winter, reminded them of the snowdrop-filled woodlands of home.

One that is almost as inexpensive as the common snowdrop is *G. elwesii*, a native of Turkey. This is very large-flowered, tall, early and sweetly scented; good for picking and bringing indoors during January. In fact, some of my bulbs start to bloom in late December with *Cyclamen coum*, and the last flowers are still popping up in early April; but then all these are variable in their flowering time, and the more you have (as with *Cyclamen hederifolium*) the longer you will enjoy them. This species seems more tolerant of full sun than the rest, which generally prefer dry shade, and mine do well even in the hottest and driest places —even in the rock garden. By the way, you will often find *elwesii* sold in garden centres as 'large single snowdrop'.

I did say that I would ration myself to just a few snowdrops, but I cannot forego a brief mention of a superb snowdrop-like flower, *Leucojum vernum*. This is a stunner for late winter, flowering with the snowdrops and at first glance looking very much like a particularly large-flowered species or variety of these. They are related, but on closer inspection the crystalline white flowers of the leucojum are a quite different bell shape, with a striking green spot to the tip of each broad petal. It likes the same sort of dry shade as the snowdrops, with plenty of peat or compost in the soil.

The winter aconite, *Eranthis hyemalis*, is good for planting with snowdrops and cyclamen under trees and shrubs, adding a bright touch of yellow to the display in February and March. I have recently noticed tubers being advertised in the gardening press, along with the common snowdrop, 'in the green', and this would certainly be a better way to establish them, since they dislike being dried out as much as do the snowdrops. 'Guinea Gold' is even better, a richer yellow and with bronze-tinted new leaves, but unfortunately seldom seen; snap it up if you are lucky enough to find it on offer.

Dwarf bulbous irises are a delight in winter, starting with the sky-blue *Iris histrioides* 'Major' in early January, followed by the canary-yellow *I. danfordiae*, and then the blue, violet and purple-red varieties of *I. reticulata* in February and early March. They need very well-drained conditions and are best in sandy soil in the rock garden

Leucojum vernum, *a lovely snowdrop-like bulb for late winter; this is a particularly robust form*, L. vernum vagneri.

or raised bed. Some tend to exhaust themselves or split up into small non-flowering bulbils after the first year, but deep planting and feeding with potash will help to keep them blooming regularly. The ones that flower year after year for me, without splitting up too much, include *histrioides* 'Major', the pale blue *reticulata* 'Cantab' and the deep blue *reticulata* 'Harmony'.

Spring bulbs

There is a wide range of very neat spring-flowering crocus species (and their varieties) available as a far more refined alternative to the rather gross large-flowered Dutch crocus. Most popular, and deservedly so, are the extremely free-flowering blue, yellow, cream and white *Crocus chrysanthus* varieties, each corm producing as many as five blooms in February and March.

Crocus ancyrensis is another free-flowerer, with masses of rich orange-yellow early blooms, and vigorous in growth. But my all-time favourite, lovely in rock gardens and raised beds, is *C. biflorus alexandri*, pure glistening white inside with a glossy purple exterior. *C. minimus* is another that I enjoy very much, ideal for a rock garden with its neat little blooms, violet-blue inside and feathered purple on the backs of the petals. The Grecian *C. sieberi* is a strong grower, good for its golden-throated lilac-blue flowers, 'Firefly' being a larger variety. As with the snowdrops, I could go on for ever, but I'll end with the popular *C. tommasinianus*. The pale lavender type seeds freely and may become a nuisance in a small garden, but the darker forms, 'Ruby Giant', 'Whitewell Purple' and 'Barr's Purple', tend not to seed and are content to make strong spreading clumps.

Tuberous anemones provide some valuable early colour, the neatest and most delightful being *Anemone blanda*, a dainty little thing for mixing with other spring bulbs beneath shrubs and trees; the rich blue 'Atrocaerulea' is the finest form, but there are also white and pink varieties, all blooming from February to April. Larger and even more showy is the *A. fulgens* 'St Bavo' strain. These flowers are as large as those of the popular *A. coronaria* 'de Caen' strain, yet more refined and elegant with a colour range that usually

includes a good proportion of pastel pinks and lilac-blues as well as intense mauves and scarlet-reds. I also grow *A. fulgens* 'Annulata Grandiflora', a particularly bright scarlet form with a buff-yellow eye. These provide colour later in the season, during April and May.

Bulb catalogues offer a wide range of dwarf daffodils ideal for the small garden. Quite apart from the fact that you can squeeze in more, in a wider range and for different flowering times and different situations, these smaller narcissi do not produce anything like the large, untidy foliage of the tallest trumpet varieties.

For early colour in the rock garden and under shrubs, the diminutive hoop petticoat daffodil, *Narcissus bulbocodium*, is a charming choice; so, too, are *N. asturiensis* (the tiniest trumpet, at just 7.5 cm or 3 ins tall), *N. cyclamineus* (best in a shady corner with plenty of peat), *N. juncifolius* and the white Angels' tears daffodil, *N. triandrus albus*. The wild jonquil, *N. jonquilla*, is superb for late colour and fragrance, its neat shallow-cupped blooms being richly scented; 'Baby Moon' is a very free-flowering and late variety.

There are also some wonderful small trumpet hybrids available, all far neater than the commonly-planted large trumpets. The hybrids from *N. cyclamineus* are all lovely, with their narrow trumpets and slightly turned-back petals; 'February Gold' has to be the very best small-garden daffodil, always free with its blooms, produced on sturdy 25 cm (10 in) stems in February and March, and very vigorous. 'Dove Wings' is taller, white with a primrose cup, and 'Tête-a-Tête' is very dwarf, with two yellow trumpets to a stem. Of the *N. triandrus* hybrids, all with elegant, dangling small-cupped blooms, the lemon-yellow 'Liberty Bells' and the white 'Thalia' are superb, both late flowering.

Chionodoxas, or glory of the snow, to give them their poetic common name, provide brilliant patches of sky-blue in the spring garden, and I like to have them everywhere in variety; not just the popular *luciliae* and *gigantea*, but also the very deep gentian-blue *sardensis* and the dainty

Tulipa tarda, a very reliable yellow-and-white flowered species.

tmoli. And the deep Prussian-blue *Scilla siberica* 'Spring Beauty' goes well with small yellow daffodils like 'February Gold'.

For late spring, the dwarf tulip species provide a colourful show without taking up much space, and they may be left in the ground all year provided it is reasonably well-drained. *Tulipa tarda* is easy and eye-catching with its yellow-centred white star flowers. Put this in a sunny spot where it will grow up through other plants in the border, to give some support to its rather floppy stems. *T. praestans* 'Fusilier' is also a good small-garden bulb, very neat and extremely generous with up to five glowing orange-scarlet blooms to a stem (even two or three bulbs will make a good show). For the rock garden or raised bed, *T. linifolia* is a stunning dwarf with deep red flowers. And finally, one of the most desirable of tulip species is the bright orange-red *T. sprengeri*; wonderful for a little splash of late colour, and flowering towards the end of May after all the others.

The lily-like erythroniums are very classy plants for late spring, the yellow 'Pagoda' and the large-flowered 'White Beauty' being the strongest growers and the showiest, their nodding blooms carried above handsome broad leaves. Both enjoy shade, and plenty of peat or compost where the soil is on the dry side.

Fritillarias have enjoyed increasing popularity of recent years, and there are dozens of species available. The one that should be in every garden is our dainty native snake's head fritillary, *F. meleagris*; easy in shade where not too dry. The nodding chequered bell flowers vary from deep violet-purple to pure white; watch out for named forms like the snowy white 'Aphrodite' and the rich purple 'Orion'.

Finally, the deep rose-red *Cyclamen repandum* looks good in late spring carpeting the dry ground beneath shrubs; its thin leaves tend to scorch if it gets too much sun, so tuck it into a really shady spot right under a shrub.

Erythronium 'White Beauty', flowering beneath shrubs in spring.

Colourful summer bulbs

For this season, I would recommend lilies above all else; they really make a wonderful show and I do not think any garden could have too many of them.

Lilies are not as difficult to please as many people seem to think, or at least most of them are not. The one essential is good drainage so that the fleshy bulbs are not sitting in soggy soil during winter. That does not mean digging a deep hole and sitting the lilies on a pile of sand or grit, as is so often recommended—do that, and the sand will simply act as a sump into which water will seep from the surrounding soil, making the poor bulbs wetter than ever during their winter rest.

Where the soil is heavy, mix lashings of sharp sand or grit thoroughly into the planting site, along with plenty of peat, to improve the drainage generally rather than just in the bottom of the planting hole. And at the same time add a good dose of John Innes Base or Blood, Fish and Bone fertiliser. The peat is as important as the drainage, since all lilies enjoy summer moisture. As for choosing planting positions, on a flat site these should ideally be raised slightly above the general garden level, raised beds being ideal, although any sunny and well-prepared border will do. Alternatively, the bulbs may be planted to grow up through small shrubs, where they will be drier in winter than in the open. All lilies like their roots to be shaded by other plants in summer, with their heads growing up into sunlight, so they are good subjects for cramming into the border. Only *Lilium martagon* will tolerate deep shade. The best time to plant is late autumn, but early spring will do.

Lilium regale is one of the most easy-going, its strongly scented white and wine-red trumpets filling the garden with fragrance in July; it will flourish in any situation and soil except the wettest. The trumpet hybrids, such as 'Royal Gold', are equally reliable, and so are the low-growing and upright-flowered hybrids like the lemon-yellow 'Destiny', and the many pendant-flowered hybrids. *L. candidum*, the white Madonna lily, is one for a hot, dry spot, preferably in a sunny wall bed. At the other extreme, as I have said, *L. martagon* likes shade, and the stunning white form of this looks particularly good in a shady corner.

There are also some wonderful Scottish-raised lilies now becoming widely available, all tough but very elegant. The best of them are pendant-flowered with recurving petals, the blooms carried in an elegant pyramidal fashion up the stem. The varieties that have done well with me over the last three or four years include the deep wine-red 'Theseus', the fragrant pink 'Eros', and the orange-red 'Orestes'. None of them mind lime in the soil, in fact none of the lilies mentioned so far do, although they all appreciate some peat, as already mentioned, to hold summer moisture and lighten the soil. An address for obtaining these Scottish lilies is given at the end of the book.

Oriental lilies, such as the red or pink flowered *L. speciosum*, the white-flowered *L. auratum* and the many hybrids between these, must have lime-free soil, peat bed treatment or a tub of lime-free compost. They bloom in late summer and early autumn and are some of the loveliest of garden flowers.

Finally, a very easy yet handsome lily for late colour. *L. henryi* is a tall-growing pendant-flowered species with bright orange blooms in August and September; it is happy on limy soil and very long-lived.

Of the gladioli, I love the hardy species *Gladiolus byzantinus* for its 60 cm (2 ft) spikes of deep wine-red flowers in June. There is no need to lift this one for frost-free winter storage; plant it deep in well-enriched soil in a sunny spot, and leave it to multiply. The dwarf pink and white *G. nanus* hybrids are also lovely, no more than 60 cm (2 ft) tall and with flowers more elegant than the larger varieties so widely planted, but of course these are tender; put them in during April, and lift for storage in autumn.

Galtonia candicans, the summer hyacinth, is fairly hardy if planted at least 15 cm (6 ins) deep in a warm sheltered spot, and its 90 cm (3 ft) spires of drooping creamy-white scented bells are a delight in late summer and early autumn. Dutch irises are popular hardy bulbs for early summer, but whenever possible it is best to buy and plant selected colour forms, rather than the mixtures so often offered; a bold patch of one colour is far lovelier than a bitty collection of different hues. Alternatively, buy a mixture and sort out the different colours into separate clumps. The larger-flowered white, blue, pink and purple bulbous English irises which flower later, in July, are very lovely, quite hardy and easy; try a few if you see them offered.

The crocosmias mentioned in my chapter on hardy perennials do, of course, grow from corms and are often listed in the spring lists of mail-order bulb firms. These, as I have said, are marvellous for late summer and autumn. Finally, one of my favourite tender summer bulbs is *Tigridia pavonia*, the peacock flower from Mexico and Peru; smashing large iris-like flowers in brilliant shades of red and yellow on 45 cm (18 in) stems, from July to September.

9
Temporary Plants for Summer

This will be a very short chapter since, as I stated in Chapter One, in a small garden it does not pay to rely too much on temporary summer plants which will later leave ugly gaps and necessitate continual replanting.

I use some of the more elegant hardy annuals, for three very good reasons. Firstly, they do not need to be raised under glass (in very small gardens there is little space for a greenhouse) and they can be sown direct into the garden. Secondly, many of them are comparatively tough plants from hot, arid climates and will look after themselves without too much attention; indeed, some will happily seed themselves about even on dry, stony banks. And thirdly, most of these hardy annuals are less over-bred and 'improved' than some of the more tender types; they retain much of the elegance of wild flowers and therefore fit very well into the mixed border and into an informal garden style. I also stick to strains of single colours, rather than mixtures, since in my view this always gives a much more pleasing effect.

I particularly like the drought-resistant Californian poppies, the eschscholzias, so good for dry, sunny corners. I grow a single-flowered strain of *E. californica* which varies only from deepest yellow to orange-yellow and produces its poppy-like flowers endlessly from June to October on 25 cm (10 in) stems. And my strain of *E. caespitosa*, a dwarf plant at just 15 cm (6 ins) tall, is a pale lemon-yellow. Both have handsome ferny foliage and will seed around.

Nemophila menziesii, commonly known as baby blue eyes, is another Californian native and good on dry soils, in sun or partial shade; sky-blue flowers with a white centre are produced above low-growing feathery foliage over a long period. *Linum grandiflorum* rubrum is the scarlet flax, a hardy annual species with brilliant red flowers on slender 30 cm (1 ft) high stems from June to August; another useful one for filling empty corners, particularly those that are sunny and dry.

Sweet peas are also a favourite with me—the old-fashioned strains with highly fragrant blooms. They are superb both as climbers and as trailing plants to grow over retaining walls and in hanging baskets and tubs.

Other dainty hardy annuals to consider include the blue cornflower, *Centaurea cyanus*, available in both tall and dwarf strains; and the viscarias or rose of heaven, more correctly strains of *Silene coeli-rosa*, with flowers that vary widely from pale pastel hues to rich reds and purples (keep an eye out for single-colour strains).

I also like *Gypsophila elegans* (popularly known as baby's breath), with its elegant branching stems bearing clouds of delicate white flowers so frequently used in flower arrangements and bouquets; it can also be had in shell pink. It blooms from May to September.

Dimorphotheca aurantiaca (star of the veldt) is a very bright little flower, like a large daisy in hot shades of orange, yellow or salmon-pink. It must have a hot and sunny spot. Here again, look out for single-colour seed strains for best effect.

Although these hardy annuals are easily sown and grown in the open ground, they will do better if the sowing site is prepared, with a little moist peat and fertiliser raked in. Watering during dry spells in spring and early summer will encourage the best results, and an occasional liquid feed will give the young plants a real boost. And, of course, if you can find the time to remove dead flowers during summer, the display will be more prolonged (but leave some of the later dead-heads, if you want to collect seed for the following year).

10
Climbing Plants

The best climbers for small gardens are those that offer more than one feature, such as bright flowers plus a strong fragrance or handsome foliage; or those which have attributes that are of interest in different seasons. These are points to bear in mind when you are buying. And do not forget, as I mentioned in Chapter Three, that you can mix climbers, allowing them to intermingle on the same piece of wall or fence to obtain flowers and interest at different times.

Reliable evergreens are few and far between, but the ivies are useful for year-round cover on ugly walls and fences, particularly in constant shade. The strong-growing Japanese honeysuckle, *Lonicera japonica*, is semi-evergreen—mine held much of its foliage even through the 1984 –85 winter freeze-up and, although it was rather bedraggled towards the end, it soon burst into new growth. 'Halliana' is the variety usually offered, the flowers opening creamy-white and turning yellow, the display continuous from June to October and the sweet scent filling the whole garden; one that I could not recommend too highly, it will tolerate some shade and quickly covers ugly features.

Equally fragrant is the white jasmine, *Jasminum officinale*, a vigorous and hardy climber as long-flowering as the honeysuckle, from June to September.

Of the clematis, I particularly like *Clematis montana* 'Tetrarose', a mass of deep lilac-rose blooms up to 7.5 cm (3 ins) across in May, against handsome bronze-green foliage; 'Elizabeth' is a soft pink variety, also large-flowered. Both are very vigorous and easy. For later colour, there are *C. orientalis* and *C. tangutica*, both with attractive nodding yellow flowers from August to October, followed by silky seed-heads. It would be interesting to combine one of these with one of the spring-flowering *montana* varieties, the two intermingling and giving a double display, the dark foliage of montana contrasting with the paler, deeply-cut leaves of the autumn species. For something that will never get very large or tall, the violet-blue *C. macropetala* and the blue *C. alpina* would be good choices, both spring-flowering.

Virginia creepers can be a bit of a pest once they get a hold, their clinging shoots romping over the largest walls, trying to obscure windows and scrambling over gutters. But the ornamental grape vine, *Vitis vinifera* 'Brandt', is less rampant and more easily controlled; good for autumn colour, its large leaves turn crimson, pink and orange, with the bonus of edible black grapes. Hardy wine-making grape varieties, suitable for eating as well as for home plonk-production, are also good on a sunny wall or fence, as are the handsome scarlet runner beans; but more on these in Chapter Twelve.

Another useful foliage climber that I like very much indeed is the golden-leaved hop, *Humulus lupulus* 'Aureus'. This is herbaceous, dying down to the ground in winter, but it is a fast grower which will quickly shoot back up to 2.5 m (8 ft) each year, and it is useful as a summer screen. The bright golden-yellow leaves look good scrambling over a fence, through a hedge or up an old tree.

The Chilean flame creeper, *Tropaeolum speciosum*, is an uncommon herbaceous climber which will twine its way through a hedge or shrub in summer, the brilliant flame-scarlet flowers making a superb show from July to September, followed by bright blue berries. This needs to be planted on the cool north side of a hedge or shrub, deep in soil liberally laced with peat and watered during dry weather in spring and early summer. It is best in the cooler areas of the north and the moist regions of the west of Britain, but I manage to grow it in my windy, hot, dry and limy garden; not as well as I have seen it in cooler gardens, but well enough for me. It is certainly worth trying, since it is such a stunning flower.

Finally, the perennial sweet peas, lovely herbaceous climbers for training on walls or fences, or for scrambling through spring-flowering shrubs to brighten them up in summer. *Lathyrus latifolius*, an old cottage garden flower, can be had in white, pink or rose-red, growing to about 2.5 m (8 ft)—a beautiful sight. *L. grandiflorus* grows to about 1.5 m (5 ft) with spectacular large crimson-red pea flowers. Both are easily raised from seed. Unfortunately, they are not scented.

A vigorous semi-evergreen climber, ideal for camouflaging ugly fences and walls: Lonicera japonica 'Halliana', *the fragrant, creamy-yellow summer flowering Japanese honeysuckle, seen here still blooming in late October.*

11
Hedging Plants

I have already discussed hedges and hedging plants to some extent in earlier chapters, so I shall keep this brief. Firstly, I should like to repeat my praise of beech as a superb (perhaps unbeatable) hedging plant of great character. Reasonably fast-growing yet easily trimmed to a neat formal shape, it has wonderful fresh green spring foliage, a solid summer screen, and beautiful russet autumn leaves which last right through winter (and birds love to nest in it, too)—an 'evergreen' screen without the dull same-all-year-round look of so many true evergreens. I should like to see it being planted as widely as the ubiquitous 'leylandii'; our streets and gardens would be more interesting and attractive for it.

I have also briefly mentioned flowering hedges. These do take up a little more room, since they cannot be trimmed as neatly or as regularly as formal non-flowering hedges; but, then, you are getting two benefits from one feature: a screen plus colour. The sweetly scented *Rosa rugosa* makes a lovely hedge—a colourful screen, and fragrance too. It can be kept reasonably neat by pruning when flowering is over. This is easily and inexpensively obtainable as a hedging plant.

Berberis darwinii makes a fairly neat, slow-growing and upright evergreen flowering hedge with small glossy leaves and yellow or orange-yellow flowers in April and May. This, too, can be trimmed once a year after flowering. *Cotoneaster franchetii* is another good evergreen hedger, or semi-evergreen at least; it can be kept fairly neat by pruning after flowering, removing as much of the vigorous new shoots as possible while leaving as many berry clusters as possible.

Many low-growing shrubs will make very small hedges suitable for edging borders, dividing up the garden into interesting compartments, or even as low boundary hedges. Box is the classic shrub for small hedges and very attractive when trimmed to shape. *Buxus sempervirens*, the common box, slowly makes a very neat hedge of about 90 cm to 1.25 m (3 to 4 ft), eventually more after many years. *B. sempervirens* 'Suffruticosa' is the even slower dwarf box used for border edgings. Some of the dwarf berberis mentioned in the shrub chapter are also good, notably the purple-leaved deciduous *Berberis thunbergii* 'Atropurpurea' (1.25 m or 4 ft) and the dwarf variety 'Atropurpurea Nana' (45 cm or 18 ins). Of flowering shrubs, the potentillas, hebes and lavenders are good.

Do not forget what I said in Chapter Three about mixed hedges for variety; and I do not mean simply a mixture of flowering and non-flowering plants, or evergreens and deciduous, but perhaps a climber or two as well, to ramble through the hedge.

That may sound rather odd at first, but country hedgerows are seldom all one thing (even if they were originally planted that way) and they are all the more lovely and interesting for it; why should we not take a small leaf out of nature's book?

Dwarf box makes an excellent border edging or a low hedge for small gardens; growing here with snowdrops and cyclamen foliage.

114

12
Fruit and Vegetables

It is amazing how many fruits and vegetables can be grown in a small garden without having to set aside a separate patch for them, if they are planted amongst the flowers.

Let us look at fruit first. For a start, a standard apple tree could perhaps be substituted for an ornamental tree, to give lovely spring blossom plus the bonus of a delicious crop. But remember that for heavy cropping, most apples need to cross-pollinate with another tree of a different variety growing nearby and flowering around the same time. In a small space this problem could be solved by growing another variety (or two) as a very dwarf bush (see Useful Addresses for suppliers). The latest dwarfing rootstocks really do make apples a possibility for even the tiniest of gardens; bushes on M27 stock will grow very slowly to less than 1.5 m (5 ft) in height with a 1.25 m (4 ft) spread, suitable for either the borders or tubs. They can also be grown as miniature cordons, tied in to a low fence or wall, perhaps. The one thing to bear in mind is that apples on these ultra-dwarfing rootstocks must have well-prepared soil, or a good potting compost and regular feeding if grown in a tub.

Family apple trees are also available from some growers (see Useful Addresses); these have three different varieties of apple grafted onto one trunk, for good cross-pollination and a range of fruits.

Blackberries may also be grown on fences and walls, for their pretty flowers and delicious fruits; there are some good thornless varieties available, and 'Oregon Thornless' is particularly attractive with its deeply-cut, almost ferny leaves which often take on colourful autumn tints of orange

and yellow; flowers, handsome foliage, tasty fruits and autumn colour—what more could you ask for?

Outdoor grapes, too, make attractive coverings for sunny walls and fences, with their large and shapely leaves, often colouring yellow or orange in autumn. The most reliable croppers are the tough and fully hardy wine varieties, the fruits of which can either be eaten (although they are rather full of pips) or made into your own 'château bottled'. One of the most vigorous, and a heavy cropper, is 'Muller Thurgau' ('Riesling Sylvaner'). This is the grape most widely planted in commercial English vineyards, and it is commonly used in German wine production, too. I also grow the classic 'Chardonnay' grape from which the French produce such delicious Chablis. 'Seibel 13053' (or 'Cascade') is a very pretty red-wine grape with colourful autumn foliage and bright red shoots. But my most attractive vine is one that has been grown in Britain for centuries (probably introduced by the Romans): 'Wrotham Pinot', a black wine grape with the most wonderful silvery new leaves as good as any willow in spring, the woolly silver-white coating being retained even on the mature foliage. All of these can be found in garden centres or obtained by mail order.

The hardy wine-making outdoor grape variety 'Muller Thurgau' trained on a sunny wall; a vigorous and heavy-cropping variety which makes a fruity German-style wine. Here, the handsome leaves are starting to colour up in autumn.

Strawberries are handsome fruits as a border-edging near the kitchen door, and there are runnerless alpine strawberries which will sit in the border and make neat clumps with small but delicious fruit carried on tall, arching stems; the birds tend to ignore them, so there are no netting worries, and they do not suffer from the diseases that plague the large strawberries. Look out for the alpine varieties 'Baron Solemacher', 'Alexandria' and 'Yellow Alpine' (available as plants or seed). Being runnerless, they may also be planted in paving, but will need regular watering and feeding with liquid fertiliser in this situation. Plant large-fruited strawberries as pot-grown runners in late summer (before mid-August) to fruit the following year; planted in autumn or spring, they will not crop properly until their second year and will waste space in the meantime.

As for vegetables, the most attractive of all has to be the scarlet-flowered runner bean, which was originally grown purely as an ornamental summer climber before its delicious flavour and food value were discovered. Try this on sunny fences and walls; perhaps even in a tub or in the border, where it will scramble over a pyramid of canes and make a lovely feature; or perhaps climbing up a drainpipe with some garden twine for support. I have also grown it as a trailer to drape over an ugly retaining wall, and as a decorative climber to scramble through dull shrubs in summer. Sow seeds in late May or early June, and pick the beans young, when they are tender and most delicious, to encourage continued flowering and cropping (the plant will also look less like a vegetable if you do this, and more like a decorative feature).

'Scarlet Emperor' is one of the most colourful red-flowered varieties, but there is also a very attractive red-and-white one, 'Painted Lady'.

Dwarf French beans will also fit nicely into the garden, particularly the handsome purple-podded varieties like 'Royal Burgundy' (the pods turn green when cooked). Tomatoes are attractive enough in leaf and fruit not to look out of place alongside flowers, and there are some good dwarf bush varieties available, like the very neat 'Tiny Tim' which produces cherry-sized fruits and is small enough even for windowsill pots and windowboxes. Peppers (capsicums) can also look very attractive, as can courgettes with their large leaves and pretty flowers. And a quick crop of fast growers like spring onions, radishes and lettuce can be produced in a sunny corner at the back of the border where the chances are no one will notice them or realise what they are. And there are many attractive culinary herbs that look good in the border: parsley, sage, thyme, chives and rosemary, to name but a few.

Do remember that to crop well, fruits and vegetables need well-prepared soil with plenty of peat or compost and some compound fertiliser. They will also demand regular watering in dry weather, especially if grown in containers or in amongst flowering plants; and regular liquid feeding (about three times a year in spring and summer for fruits, and fortnightly for vegetables) will help to ensure good results; a high-potash liquid fertiliser is best for fruit trees and bushes, for fruiting vegetables like tomatoes, and for beans (tomato fertiliser will do for all of these).

Scarlet runner beans growing in a tub against a sunny wall. The large leaves and bright red flowers make a handsome summer feature with the bonus of a delicious crop. These are the heavy-cropping 'Scarlet Emperor', planted with an outdoor tomato, growing up an arrangement of canes and garden twine secured to hooks in the wall.

Plants for Special Conditions

Plants for shade

(D) = tolerant of dry shade beneath trees and shrubs

Anemone nemerosa (D)
Anemone blanda (D)
Anemone 'St Bavo' strain (D)
Anemone hybrida (*A. japonica*)
Aquilegia alpina
Bergenia (D)
Camellia
Colchicum (D)
Convallaria (Lily of the valley) (D)
Cotoneaster
Cyclamen (D)
Dicentra spectabilis
Epimedium (D)
Eranthis (D)
Erythronium (D)
Fatsia
Ferns
Fritillaria meleagris
Galanthus (Snowdrops) (D)
Helleborus (D)
Hosta
Lilium martagon and *L. martagon album*
Lonicera (Honeysuckle)
Mahonia
Meconopsis
Milium effusum 'Aureum'
Pieris
Primula (border types)
Primroses and Polyanthus
Pyracantha
Rhododendron and Azalea
Sarcococca (D)
Scilla (D)
Skimmia
Trillium (D)

Drought-tolerant plants for very dry, sunny areas
Anemone 'St Bavo' strain
Aubrieta
Armeria
Berberis
Chionodoxa
Colchicum
Cistus
Crocus
Cytisus
Dianthus
Eremurus
Eschscholzia
Genista
Geranium sanguineum
Hebe
Helianthemum
Hemerocallis
Hibiscus
Hypericum
Iris (dwarf spring bulbs)
Lavandula
Linum
Lilium candidum
Lilium regale
Nerine
Oenothera
Penstemon
Potentilla
Pyracantha
Thyme
Tulipa

Plants for paving and paths
Armeria caespitosa
Campanula garganica
Campanula cochlearifolia
Dianthus (esp. *D. deltoides*)
Geranium dalmaticum
Geranium sanguineum
Hypericum olympicum
Hypericum reptans
Iris unguicularis (*stylosa*)
Lithospermum diffusum (lime hater)
Penstemon pinifolius
Phlox douglasii
Phlox subulata
Thymes
Viola cornuta and *V. cornuta* 'Alba'

Plants to grow in retaining walls
Alyssum saxatile varieties
Armeria caespitosa
Aubrieta
Campanula garganica
Geranium sanguineum
Lewisia cotyledon
Penstemon pinifolius
Phlox douglasii
Phlox subulata
Primula marginata
Saxifraga (rosette-forming encrusted types; e.g.
    S. cotyledon 'Southside Seedling')

Useful
Addresses

Should you have difficulty locating any of the plants discussed in this book, the following addresses may be of some help. These include addresses of some specialist societies which may be of interest to small-garden owners.

Societies
Alpine Garden Society, Lye End Link, St John's, Woking, Surrey.

Scottish Rock Garden Club, Miss K. M. Gibb, 21 Merchiston Park, Edinburgh.

Hardy Plant Society, 10 St Barnabas Road, Emmer Green, Caversham, Reading.

All the above have annual seed exchanges through which seed of unusual and uncommon plants may often be obtained.

Suppliers
Rock plants
W. E. Th. Ingwersen Ltd, Birch Farm Nursery, Gravetye, East Grinstead, W. Sussex.

Jack Drake, Inshriach Alpine Plant Nursery, Aviemore, Inverness-shire. (*Especially autumn gentians.*)

Hartside Nursery Garden, Low Gill House, Alston, Cumbria.

The Cottage Nursery, Moortown Road, Nettleton, Caistor, Lincolnshire. (*Also uncommon dwarf bulbs.*)

Edrom Nurseries, Coldingham, Eyemouth, Berwickshire. (*Alpines.*)

Holden Clough Nurseries, Bolton-by-Bowland, Clitheroe, Lancashire.

Reginald Kaye, Waithman Nurseries, Lindeth Road, Silverdale, Lancashire. (*Alpines and ferns.*)

Lye End Nursery, Lye End Link, St John's Woking, Surrey.

Hardy perennials
Bressingham Gardens, Diss, Norfolk. (*Also alpines, heathers, dwarf conifers and dwarf shrubs.*)

Scott's Nurseries, Merriott, Somerset. (*Also trees, shrubs, fruit trees and bushes.*)

Beth Chatto, White Barn House, Elmstead Market, Colchester, Essex. (*Specialises in unusual plants.*)

Lilies
Highland Liliums, Kiltarlity, by Beauly, Inverness-shire. (*Stock includes the lovely new Scottish hybrids.*)

Walter Blom and Son, Leavesden, Watford, Herts.

Dwarf bulbs
The Cottage Nursery, Moortown Road, Nettleton, Caistor, Lincolnshire.

Avon Bulbs, Bradford-on-Avon, Wiltshire.

Broadleigh Gardens, Barr House, Bishop's Hull, Taunton, Somerset.

Trees, shrubs, roses and conifers
Hillier Nurseries, Ampfield, Romsey, Hampshire.

Notcutts Nurseries, Woodbridge, Suffolk.

Peter Beales, London Road, Attleborough, Norfolk. (*Old and shrub roses.*)

Fruit trees and bushes, vines

Chris Bowers and Sons, Whispering Trees Nurseries, Wimbotsham, Norfolk. (*Stock includes fruit trees on dwarfing rootstocks.*)

Highfield Nurseries, Whitminster, Gloucester-shire. (*Stock includes fruit trees on dwarfing rootstocks.*)

Cranmore Vineyard, Yarmouth, Isle of Wight. (*Grapevines suitable for the British climate.*)

Suggested Further Reading and Reference Books

Titles marked with an asterisk are a particularly good read, entertaining as well as informative.

The Reader's Digest Encyclopaedia of Garden Plants and Flowers, second edition 1978, The Readers Digest Association.

The Wisley Book of Gardening, edited by Robert Pearson, 1981, the Royal Horticultural Society in association with Collingridge.

The Wisley Handbooks: small, inexpensive guides to many different kinds of plants and gardening ideas, including plants for shade, gardening on lime and chalk, pruning shrubs, plans for small gardens, peat gardens, roses, rhododendrons, climbers, camellias, alpines, and much more. The Royal Horticultural Society in association with Cassell.

The Hillier Colour Dictionary of Trees and Shrubs, 1981, David and Charles.

Perennial Garden Plants by Graham Stuart Thomas, second edition 1982, J. M. Dent and Sons.

Plants for Ground-Cover by Graham Stuart Thomas, revised edition 1977, J. M. Dent and Sons.

Growing Hardy Perennials by Kenneth Beckett, 1981, Croom Helm.

Growing Irises by G. E. Cassidy and S. Linnegar, 1981, Croom Helm.

Collins' Guide to Alpine and Rock Garden Plants by Anna N. Griffith, third edition 1973, William Collins.

The Collingridge Guide to Collectors' Alpines by Royton E. Heath, 1981, Collingridge.

Alpine Gardening by Roy Elliot, 1963, Vista Books.

Alpines and Rock Plants by Will Ingwersen, 1983, J. M. Dent and Sons.

The Ingwersen Manual of Alpine Plants by Will Ingwersen, 1978, W. E. Th. Ingwersen.

Rock Plants for Small Gardens by Royton E. Heath, 1982, Collingridge.

Collins' Guide to Bulbs by Patrick M. Synge, second edition 1971, William Collins.

The Bulb Book by Martyn Rix and Roger Phillips, 1981, Pan Books.

Lilies by Carl Feldmaier, 1970, B. T. Batsford.

Growing Lilies by D. B. Fox, 1985, Croom Helm.

Growing Bulbs by Martin Rix, 1984, Croom Helm.

Growing Cyclamen by Gay Nightingale, 1982, Croom Helm.

My Garden in Spring by E. A. Bowles, reissued 1972, David and Charles.

My Garden in Summer by E. A. Bowles, reissued 1972, David and Charles.

My Garden in Autumn and Winter by E. A. Bowles, reissued 1972, David and Charles.

We Made a Garden by Margery Fish, 1983, Faber Paperbacks.

The Year-round Bulb Garden by Brian Mathew, Autumn 1986, Souvenir Press.

Index

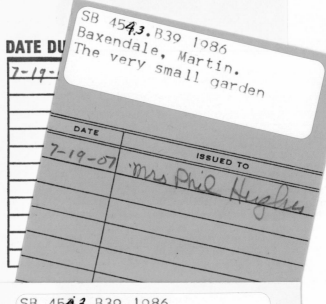